The AI Fix for Private Equity

A New Playbook for Value Creation from Pre-Deal to Exit

Mark Rogerson and Gary M Pearson

Newthistle Consulting LLC

Praise for the AI Fix for Private Equity

"Impressive work, clear enough to apply even if you are not a tech specialist, and genuinely useful in the boardroom and on the ground."
- M.A., Private Equity Partner

"The AI Fix for PE is the first book length examination of how to connect AI to value creation in portfolio companies, rich with real examples and the organisational requirements that ensure concrete benefits are delivered. Invaluable reading."
- Dr Mike Hicks, CEO, Catalysis Advisory, and author of Assessing and Strengthening Teams and Organisations

"As someone outside private equity, this was a feast: leadership lessons and practical management tactics that travel across complex organizations, including multinational environments. You will find yourself smiling, reflecting, and applying the ideas."
- Huiming Chen, Regional CFO, public biotech

Contents

EXECUTIVE SUMMARY

AI is no longer a side project. It's the primary engine of competitive advantage and value creation, both in technology and in every sector PE touches. The traditional levers, financial engineering, operational efficiency, bolt-on acquisitions, still matter, but they're being outpaced by system-level AI adoption that enables real-time sensing, decision-making, and adaptation.

The firms that win the next decade will be the ones that build AI into the *core operating system* of the business, making intelligence part of how the company runs, scales, and defends its position.

The Strategic Imperative

System-first beats feature-first. Cosmetic AI features deliver temporary efficiency but quickly commoditize. An AI-native core drives defensibility, margin expansion, and valuation uplift.

Sequence matters. Build the intelligent core first. Capture quick wins in secondary systems in parallel, but never at the expense of the foundation. Move to customer-facing differentiation only when the core is stable.

Leadership and governance decide the outcome. The biggest risks aren't technical, they're organizational. Leaders must be willing to cede control to system-led decision-making, and governance must protect value across data, models, risk, and compliance.

What This Book Delivers

Frameworks for every phase of the PE lifecycle

- **Pre-deal:** AI readiness diagnostics, due diligence checklists, leadership AI literacy assessments.
- **First 100 days:** Roadmaps for intelligent system builds, governance templates, parallel quick-win plans.

- **Grow & Scale:** Value capture playbooks, prioritization tools, governance maturity scaling.
- **Exit:** Narrative construction guides, buyer-specific evidence packs, defensibility proof points.

Dual-track execution – Building the core while delivering short-term results in secondary systems keeps momentum without starving the foundation.

Case examples – Real and illustrative scenarios showing how AI-native cores outperform feature-led approaches.

Practical Recommendations

1. **Prioritize system intelligence early.** Avoid chasing surface-level wins that undermine long-term defensibility.
2. **Defend the sequence.** Quick wins should never starve the core build of leadership attention or resources.
3. **Prepare for exit from day one.** Governance, documentation, and a credible AI narrative are not add-ons, they're part of the transformation.
4. **Manage surplus capacity deliberately.** Redeploy talent freed by AI into growth roles rather than treating them purely as cost savings.

The Payoff

Compound advantage. An AI-native core compounds defensibility, adaptability, and market agility over time, making your position harder to copy with every quarter.

Exit readiness. A well-governed, fully integrated AI core commands premium multiples and buyer confidence.

Window of opportunity. The gap between surface-level AI adoption and AI-native operations is closing. Those who act with focus and discipline now will win the premium valuations.

This isn't a book about chasing hype. It's a manual for PE operators, investors, and portfolio leaders who want to build intelligent, adaptable businesses that command premium outcomes at exit, by getting the sequence right, keeping governance tight, and building systems competitors can't easily copy.

MEET THE AUTHORS

Mark Rogerson and Gary Pearson both served as commissioned officers in the Royal Air Force, where they specialized as air traffic controllers. Their early careers were forged under pressure, managing complex, high-stakes environments where timing, clarity, and systems thinking weren't optional.

That shared foundation, part discipline, part decision science, shaped how they lead, think, and operate. After leaving the service, both went on to successful careers in technology, private equity, and executive leadership, applying the same operational rigor to boardrooms, turnarounds, and strategic transformations. Together, they bring decades of experience helping organizations move faster, think smarter, and build systems that don't just work, but compete.

Mark Rogerson MBE, spent over 20 years in the Royal Air Force before commencing a private sector career which spanned UK-based international corporates, including Serco Plc, Costain Plc and Speedy Hire Plc.

In 2015, he commenced his private equity journey as an operating partner at a UK mid-market PE Firm.

Subsequently, Mark has become a leading mid-market PE-backed Software, Technology and Business Services Chair with an exceptional track record of building and leading complex businesses. He has held 12 PE roles as Chair/Exec Chair (9 exited) and his assets have created over £1.3Bn of Enterprise Value for investors and his management teams.

Mark has a reputation for delivering market-leading enterprise value gains and exits by developing compelling and deliverable equity development strategies, organic growth , M&A (he has completed over 70 transactions), transforming business operations and building outperforming management teams. He has led boards predominantly with a technology or core software focus in many sectors, including: FM, Telco, Fleet Logistics, Field Service Management, Tax Compliance and Construction.

His PE-backed assets include: Totalmobile - Field Service Management Software; Eque2 - Construction ERP Software; Tax Systems - Tax Compliance Software; Mycomosi - Mobile Telco Assurance Software; Connexas - Fleet Management Software; Bellrock FM - Tech Enabled Business Services; OutCo FM - Tech Enabled Business Service; Pareto FM - ESG-driven Business Services.

Mark holds an MBA from the Open University and an MA from King's College London.

Mark was awarded an MBE (Member of the Most Excellent Order of the British Empire) by Her Majesty Queen Elizabeth II. The MBE is recognition of outstanding achievement or service to the United Kingdom that has had a long-term, significant impact.

Contact – mark.rogerson@mac.com

Gary Pearson is a seasoned technology CEO, board director, and former Royal Air Force officer who made the improbable leap from marine navigation to air traffic control, and from software tester to public company CEO, sometimes by design, often by sheer refusal to stay in his lane.

With over 25 years in the software and technology trenches, Gary has led turnarounds and driven growth in global markets. As CEO and COO of an ASX-listed technology company, he orchestrated a 317% EBITDA improvement, transitioned the business to a high-margin recurring revenue model, and triggered an 1100% market cap increase.

Gary is a tech startup founder, consultant, and strategist with deep domain knowledge in artificial intelligence, especially where it intersects with systems thinking, decision velocity, and organizational leverage. He is a strong advocate for rethinking strategy in the age of AI, not as a static plan, but as a dynamic system designed to learn, adapt, and deliver differentiated value at speed. His work helps boards and CEOs avoid cosmetic AI experiments and instead build core systems that can actually scale and compete.

He currently consults through NewThistle Consulting, guiding tech businesses on how to embed intelligent systems into the fabric of their operations. He is the author of *The Accidental Strategist*, which introduced the ReSCUED framework, a battle-tested approach to strategic value creation inspired by the precision and pressure of air traffic control.

Gary holds an MBA from Nottingham Trent University and has completed extensive executive education in AI, finance, governance, and systems design. He splits his time between advising, writing about strategy in an AI-native world, and calling out LinkedIn leadership platitudes with a raised eyebrow and a dry wit.

Contact: gary@newthistleconsulting.com

www.newthistle.com

FOUNDATIONS & FRAMING

Newthistle Consulting LLC

Chapter 1

OPERATOR'S FOREWORD

Private Equity (PE) firms follow well-trodden journeys and models. In the early days, value came from financial engineering. At its core, the PE model is about sequencing; building systems and financial structures that turn opportunities into enterprise value. It's about creating exits that reward both speed and discipline.

However, these traditional levers, value proposition, go-to-market, operational efficiency, and buy-and-build, are now shifting, or at the very least, being challenged.

The new value proposition, especially in software and tech-driven services, and increasingly in 'non-tech' businesses, is Artificial Intelligence. Yes, "we know," I hear you say with raised eyebrows, and we've known this for a while.

We've seen how AI is already reshaping how our portfolio companies compete, and if they will scale or stall because of this phenomenon.

Across dozens of boards and operating teams, we've seen AI adoption burn time, waste capital, and accelerate the wrong systems, all because leadership stuck to the old playbook.

Some businesses chase chatbots and ChatGPT demos, hoping to prove they are at the forefront of modernization. Others dismiss AI as too experimental, too technical, or too expensive to prioritize. In some rooms, AI gets avoided because no one wants to invest the cost, energy, or time it requires. And like anything we don't fully understand, we avoid it.

But now, in the middle of the Buzzword Bingo, the genuine opportunity is being missed.

AI is not waiting for us to figure it out. It is already shifting how industries work. In the software sector, I see Private Equity-backed businesses standing at the front edge of this change, consciously or not. This is not another hype cycle. This marks a new approach to value creation.

I co-wrote this book with Gary as a call to arms for private equity leaders, operating partners, and management teams ready to move beyond quick wins. It's for those willing to take on the system-level work that truly builds capacity, resilience, and lasting advantage..

When applied the right way, AI helps build scalable, adaptable, customer-focused systems. It expands capacity, speeds up decision-making, and creates competitive advantages that are much harder to copy.

For portfolio company executives, this is not a thought exercise. The stakes are real. Investors expect rapid, structured, and sustainable change under pressure, and I respect that it is not an easy task. AI can help, but only when built from the core of the business ecosystem, not when deployed to appease industry, client, or investor trends.

Competitors and startups can now copy products, mirror strategies, and replicate features at speed, often with fewer people and lower costs. AI-native companies are already using intelligent systems to match offerings, undercut prices, and close the gap before the market even notices.

What used to take years to reverse-engineer now takes months. Machines that never pause can do what used to require teams of analysts. What would once have taken years and millions of dollars to correct can now be done in a fraction of the time and cost.

As a result of these new dynamics, competitive edges will not last long in the modern world. As we would say in the military, a great strategy only holds until the first engagement with the enemy. It's no different now for our portfolio companies. It is the binding ecosystem of the business entity that needs to carry the company forward.

Businesses need a strategy and plan to build, create, and sustain the modern AI-driven ecosystem. The system is what will survive when the strategy needs to evolve. The system is what allows the company to pivot, to shift, to cycle through new advantages without losing momentum. The system is what makes the next value creation phase possible.

Essentially, we need to recognize that businesses today need to build and operate differently. Layering AI onto the old operating model or systems architecture misses the point. The real work is in designing an ecosystem that can evolve, expand, and adapt while in motion. It means building systems, processes, and workflows that can sense, decide, and re-prioritize in real time. Flexibility has to be embedded into the operating model from the start, not saved for emergencies.AI should not be an accessory. It should be how the company thinks and works.

This AI field guide will hopefully help to demystify AI and get the basic working principles in motion. If you take just one or two actionable insights from this, great. No one can ever implement everything at once, and it WILL take time. But, if nothing else, we hope this book and this evolution-changing topic stimulate debate pre-deal, during those impactful first 100-day, during the transformation journey, and at the most exciting point of the next investment round.

The future is not just coming. It is already underway. And those businesses that build intelligent, adaptable ecosystems with focus and speed will be the ones writing the next Private Equity success stories and driving the highest multiples. And let's be honest, that is at the heart of this, our dynamic and exciting value creation model.

Mark Rogerson, MBE MA MBA

Chapter 2

INTRODUCTION

Why AI-Native Businesses Win (And Why Companies Get Stuck)

The business is growing. The strategy appears to be working. The dashboards look good; the board is calm, and attention drifts toward cost control around the edges. A likely exit is on the horizon. When businesses, especially those early in the PE journey, start thinking about AI, the instinct is familiar: use it to automate, smooth workflows, and shave a little time and cost from the operation. The goal is to become *AI-assisted*. It seems like the right move.

It also happens to be the trap.

According to CEOs surveyed in 2025 by the IBM Institute for Business Value, only 25% of AI initiatives met ROI expectations. Fewer than 16% reached enterprise-wide rollout. Most initiatives stalled in isolated pilots, cosmetic wins, and fragmented tools that never move the needle.

That's the problem: chasing small, safe wins that protect today's margins but fail to create tomorrow's enterprise value. Shielding the bottom line isn't the same as building a premium multiple. Driving efficiency isn't the same as building a differentiated, defensible company. The real advantage comes from doing AI differently, by building systems that competitors *can't* easily copy. Systems that learn, adapt, and deliver customer experiences others can't match or even fully understand.

This separates *AI-native* companies from those simply *AI-assisted*.

But building AI-native systems doesn't just require better tools. It requires a different kind of leadership.

Most companies are still operating under a leadership model that assumes control, sequencing, and linear execution: strategy, then action; plan, then implement. But AI-native systems don't wait for leadership to approve the next step. They don't pause for steering committees or alignment meetings. They don't stand by for permission to move.

They sense, decide, and adapt while they run.

The more complex the business, the more this matters, and the less traditional leadership structures can cope. The volume and velocity of decisions now outpace the human chain of command. Delegation helps, but it just moves the bottleneck. Even strong executive teams crack under the weight of siloed priorities, partial information, and communication lag.

That's why the leadership shift matters. The role of the leader is no longer to control the system, it's designing and managing it.

AI, when embedded into the decision architecture of the business, becomes more than a tool. It becomes the infrastructure. It supports alignment, identifies friction, surfaces what matters when it matters, and allows the organization to operate at system speed, even when the leader isn't in the room.

The human role doesn't disappear, it sharpens. Judgment, trust, motivation, ethics, coherence: these remain irreplaceable and human. But the system, the decision flow, the sense-and-respond loop, and the structural clarity has to evolve.

The future belongs to leaders who can build systems that move intelligently without them.

That's where value lives now.

The goal is still clear: increase enterprise value and maximize the exit multiple. Margins matter. Operational discipline matters. But those are the starting line. The businesses of the future, the ones that stand out at exit, will:

- Scale intelligently
- Price dynamically
- Deliver unique customer experiences

This isn't a roadmap for faster reporting cycles or minor efficiency gains. It's a blueprint for a version of the business that grows, defends, and sells at a premium.

Efficiency is expected. Differentiation drives the multiple. Sequencing makes it work.

Doing AI differently starts with a mindset. The chapters ahead will walk through:

- How to introduce AI into a private equity-owned software business

- How to design intelligent systems that don't just optimize old processes but unlock new ones
- How to create AI-native differentiation that buyers will pay for
- How to communicate this strategy to boards, investors, and buyers in a way that builds confidence, not resistance

This book will help:

- **Private equity partners and principals** tie AI differentiation directly to valuation impact
- **Operating partners** build growth engines, and capture operational leverage without blowing up risk
- **Deal teams** separate real AI-native value from surface automation stories during diligence
- **Portfolio executives** build systems that drive stickiness, pricing power, and defensible growth, not just cost savings
- **Portfolio chairs s**teer boards toward AI strategies that balance near-term returns with long-term defensibility

Some businesses will start this journey. Few will finish it. Most will take the easy path, layering AI onto legacy systems and calling it innovation. Some will build systems that can think, adapt, and scale while they run.

The easy path is crowded. The hard path is open.

The hard path is where value lives.

Chapter 3

CRUNCHBASE

From Static Database to Intelligence Engine

When Jager McConnell walked into the Crunchbase office on his first day as CEO, he could feel the contradiction in the air. The brand was everywhere, cited in pitch decks, scraped by competitors, bookmarked by VCs, but the business behind it was stalling. Revenue was flat, subscription growth was anemic, and the product itself hadn't evolved beyond being a well-structured, if static, repository of company profiles (TechCrunch, 2016).

The problem wasn't obscurity. Everyone knew Crunchbase. The problem was that everyone also knew they could get much of its value for free. Competitors mined the open data, wrapped it in sleeker interfaces, and sold it back to the very market Crunchbase had cultivated.

Spotting the Hidden Advantage

Before making any bold moves, McConnell commissioned a deep operational review. The findings were both humbling and energizing: the company's coverage breadth, the raw number of startups listed, wasn't what made it unique. Its real moat was in relationships. Years of trust with founders, accelerators, and early-stage investors meant Crunchbase had proprietary insight into private companies before they hit the mainstream radar (Forbes,2017).

The real advantage would be getting smarter, not just getting bigger.

The First 100 Days: Rebuilding the Core

If you want to change how a company works, you start with what slows it down. McConnell's first priority was speed. At the time, it could take 21 days for new funding data to appear on the platform, a lifetime in venture timelines. Engineers were drowning in manual ingestion tasks, manually verifying PDFs and news clippings (Crunchbase, 2017).

The fix was neither glamorous nor headline-grabbing: automate the data pipeline. By deploying AI-powered parsing tools and workflow orchestration, time-to-publish fell from 21 days to 48 hours. Internally, it was a morale win; externally, it signaled that Crunchbase could keep pace with the industry it was tracking.

> "We went from reporting history to predicting it."
> - McConnell in an internal all-hands (Business Powerhouse,n.d.).

Turning Data into Foresight

With the plumbing fixed, attention shifted to the product vision. The insight that transformed the roadmap was deceptively simple: users didn't come to Crunchbase to read data; they came to make better bets. That meant turning raw information into predictive intelligence.

An NLP-driven model was trained to surface "likely to fund" companies based on behavioral and market signals, hiring patterns, stealth domain registrations, early job postings, that pointed to imminent capital raises (SalesTechStar, n.d.). Premium subscribers got the feature first. It was an instant differentiator. Not only could users see what had happened, they could see what was likely to happen next.

The bet paid off. Within the first quarter of release, retention among premium users improved by 23%, and upsell rates climbed sharply (Regie.ai, n.d.).

Securing Defensibility

AI brought speed and insight, but it also brought a looming risk: being copied. The team addressed this head-on by signing exclusivity agreements with accelerator programs and investment networks, securing first-access rights to their deal flow. This was no longer just data anyone could scrape, it was proprietary intelligence.

Preparing the Equity Story

By the time the board began considering a liquidity event, Crunchbase was a different company. The narrative had shifted from "large public dataset" to "predictive market intelligence engine," a category with much higher multiples (PitchBook, 2022).

McConnell insisted that every AI feature be tied to a measurable business impact. Churn reduction, subscription uplift, market share gains, these became proof points in the exit deck.

> "Buyers don't pay for potential; they pay for proof they can touch."
>
> — McConnell to his leadership team (Roland Berger, n.d.).

Results That Spoke in Multiples

Over the course of three years:

- ARR tripled.
- Churn dropped to historic lows.
- Predictive AI features accounted for 40% of upsell conversions.

Proprietary agreements protected the company's most valuable datasets.

When the company entered final-stage negotiations, buyers weren't valuing it as a static database. They were valuing it as a SaaS intelligence platform with a growing moat, sticky customers, and defensible IP, exactly the transformation the turnaround had been designed to achieve.

From One Story to Your Story

Crunchbase's turnaround wasn't magic. It wasn't luck. It was the result of deliberate moves made under pressure, each one anchored in a clear understanding of where AI could create value that others couldn't copy. It began with seeing what the data could become, not just what it was. It accelerated when quick wins bought the time and trust needed to take bigger swings. And it finished with a clear equity story that buyers could verify, trust, and pay a premium for.

The path ahead for you may look different. Your company may be sitting on a stronger foundation, or it may be under more strain. Your market might move slower, or it might shift overnight. The details change, but the sequence holds: see the real advantage, secure it fast, build on it, and turn it into something a buyer, or competitor, can't dismiss.

In the pages that follow, this book breaks that sequence into actionable phases. Each phase has its own risks, common missteps, and leverage points.

Where the Crunchbase story shows the outcome, the next chapters show the method. You'll find the questions to ask before you buy, the governance guardrails to prevent expensive mistakes, the playbooks for early wins, the metrics that prove impact, and the positioning tactics that can turn a multiple from acceptable to exceptional.

This is where inspiration turns into execution. The boardroom conversations you'll have six months from now will be shaped by what you do in the next six weeks. And, as Crunchbase proved, when you line up the right steps in the right order, transformation moves from possibility to inevitability.

References:

Business Powerhouse (n.d.) Crunchbase CEO Jager McConnell in Exclusive Interview: AI is Now Necessary for All Companies, It's Not Even Choice.

https://www.business-powerhouse.com/crunchbase-ceo-jager-mcconnell-in-exclusive-interview-ai-is-now-necessary-for-all-companies-its-not-even-choice

Crunchbase (2017) Crunchbase speeds up data publishing with automation.

https://about.crunchbase.com/blog/automation/

Forbes (2017) What Makes Signal Unique in Startup Data.

https://www.forbes.com/sites/startupdata

PitchBook (2022) Valuation Trends in SaaS Intelligence Firms.

https://pitchbook.com/news/reports

Regie.ai (n.d.) How Crunchbase used Regie.ai to unlock $200Kin untapped pipeline.

https://www.regie.ai/customers/crunchbase

Roland Berger (n.d.) Unlocking AI's True Potential in Private Equity Value Creation.

https://www.rolandberger.com/en/Insights/Publications

SalesTechStar (n.d.) Crunchbase Declares Historical Data Dead, Relaunches as an AI-Powered Predictions Engine with up to 95% Accuracy.

https://salestechstar.com/sales-engagement/crunchbase-declares-historical-data-dead-relaunches-as-an-ai-powered-predictions-engine-with-up-to-95-accuracy/

TechCrunch (2016) Crunchbase Struggles on Subscription Front.

https://techcrunch.com

Chapter 4

AI IN THE FOUR PHASES OF THE PE DEAL

Core Concepts and Critical Groundwork for What's Next

This isn't a novel, and it's not a theoretical framework to admire from a distance. It's a field manual.

It's for operators, investors, and executives deciding under pressure. Whether you're a few weeks from signing, elbow-deep in execution, or shaping the exit story, this guide focuses on what matters, pulling the levers that create actual business value. Not buzzwords. Not AI theater. The chapters track the private equity lifecycle, from sourcing to sale. We break it down into four phases:

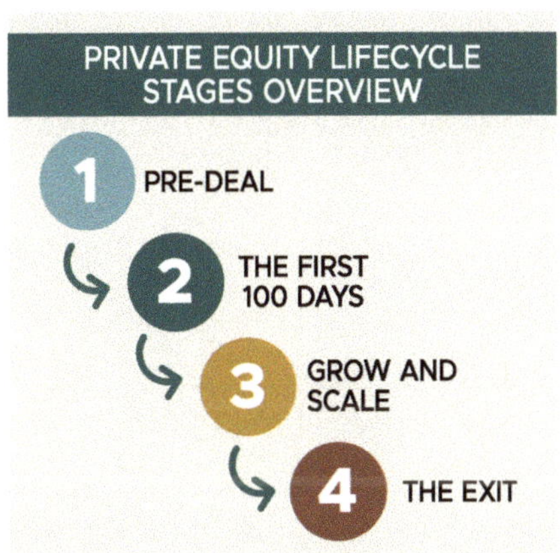

Phase 1: Pre-Deal

Diagnose, Design, and Validate System Potential

Phase 2: First 100 Days

Build the Intelligent Systems and Run the Dual-Track

Phase 3: Grow & Scale

Differentiate, Expand, and Optimize the Right Way

Phase 4: The Exit & Equity Story

Prove, Defend, and Position for Premium Value

Throughout these chapters, you'll find references to practical, downloadable worksheets, and templates that help translate ideas into action. We introduce the worksheets at the point where they are most useful, so the transition from insight to action is seamless. For those who prefer to explore the tools up front, the full worksheet library is available at www.theaifix.online

The Ground Rules

Before exploring the four phases of the private equity deal, let's establish some ground rules. Without these foundations, everything that follows becomes a checklist instead of a coherent strategy.

People rarely build systems that deliver real value in a rush. They use discipline, sequencing, and the courage to say no when the board is begging for fast savings. These foundations aren't speed bumps; they're what separate businesses that build intelligent systems from businesses that automate themselves into expensive corners.

Skip these, and you'll spend the next eighteen months explaining to increasingly impatient investors why the AI initiative that looked so promising in the deck isn't moving the needle.

Chapter 5

STOP!

Before Spending, Know What Could Blow Up

Before the AI pilot gets green-lit, the enterprise license gets signed, or someone in marketing drafts press releases about your "AI-powered transformation," take a deliberate pause.

We've seen this movie before. A new technology bursts onto the scene. AI dominates meetings, budgets get approved, and no one stops to ask, "Should this happen?" Six months later, the system behaves unpredictably. Key staff avoid taking ownership, and only the intern, who wasn't present during the approval stages, understands how the system works.

AI may not eat anyone, but it can definitely bite. In the words of Dr. Ian Malcolm (Jurassic Park): "Your scientists were so preoccupied with whether they could that they didn't stop to think if they should."

Critical Checks Before Pulling the Trigger:

License Terms & Vendor Stability

That "open-source" AI model that looks promising? Read the fine print. Plenty of tools claim to be "free" only to discover post-deployment that they come with usage restrictions that don't fit the business model, or worse, create liabilities.

- Can it be used in commercial products without revenue-sharing clauses?
- What happens if the vendor disappears in 12 months? The AI landscape is littered with startups burning cash faster than they can raise it.
- Who owns the training data and any customized or fine tuned models?
- Is there a vendor indemnification clause that kicks in when the AI results in a lawsuit?

Token-Based Cost Structure: The Invisible Running Meter

Generative AI platforms don't charge like traditional SaaS tools. Most operate on a token-based pricing model, tiny units of language used during prompts and responses. The more tokens users burn, the higher the cost.

But:

Most businesses don't know what a token is, let alone how many they're consuming.

Ask:

- Do we understand how token billing works? Can we predict usage patterns across features or customer types?
- Have we modeled token consumption per transaction, per user, or per month?
- Is our current SaaS pricing model (flat rate, tiered, usage-based) enough to cover these AI operating costs, or are we bleeding margin?
- If usage spikes, who absorbs the cost? Us or the customer?
- Do we have a plan to pass token costs through to customers without creating billing confusion or sticker shock?

Treat tokens like a raw material. Giving it away without tracking consumption isn't a business model, it's a subsidy for someone else's compute bill.

AI doesn't just add capability; it adds cost complexity. Don't wait for the invoice to find out what was overlooked or trapped.

Security & Privacy

Every AI system learns from data. The more it learns, the better it gets. But ask yourself:

- Can we source the data we need?
- Where is sensitive data stored and who can access it?
- Can the vendor use your data to improve their models for competitors?
- What happens when compliance auditors come knocking with questions about customer data?

Governance & Risk

Does this align with existing AI policies? If you don't have any policies, that's the first red flag.

- Who's accountable when the AI makes a decision that costs you customers or attracts regulatory attention?
- Is there a failsafe for unexpected issues?

AI Without Governance is a liability. Governance isn't bureaucracy, it's insurance. And like insurance, everyone hates paying for it until they need it.

Companies rushing into AI miss a critical step: Securing the business before growing it. They treat AI tools like deterministic calculators when they're actually probabilistic engines running on external infrastructure with opaque data handling policies.

The risks aren't hypothetical. They're happening right now:

- A manufacturing company's internal planning documents showed up in a competitor's ChatGPT session.
- A healthcare organization triggered HIPAA violations (Healthcare privacy for our non-USA readers) by using patient data in AI tools "just to shortcut testing."
- An AI coding assistant inadvertently shared a financial services firm's proprietary trading algorithms.

Without a risk and governance plan, the business is one careless prompt away from a compliance nightmare.

Removing AI from an organization is harder, slower, and far more expensive than its implementation. Do the risk analysis like your bonus depends on it, because it does.

Chapter 6

SYSTEM LEADERSHIP AND DECISION AUTHORITY

Guarding the Ecosystem from Distractions

An intelligent Ecosystem is more than a technical build. It's a leadership commitment, and that commitment gets tested the moment priorities collide.

Failure rarely comes from missing tools or missing talent. It comes when leadership lets the system drift, chasing what is easy to finish, what looks good in a presentation, or what relieves this quarter's pressure.

That's the mistake.

Leadership teams get pulled toward isolated automations, cosmetic dashboards, or initiatives that promise immediate recognition but deliver no structural strength. These efforts consume resources, stretch cross-functional teams, and create noise that feels like progress, but they don't build intelligent capacity.

Defend the AI strategy. Not passively, aggressively.

Someone must own the system's integrity. Someone must have the authority to say, "That's a distraction. That's not where we're going."

Decision rights must be clear:

- Who approves shifts in AI development priorities?
- Who ensures system-led decisions are acceptable, supported, and operationalized across functions?
- Who defends the system's core design when external pressure demands early results?

Without these answers, the work fragments. AI becomes a collection of disconnected experiments. The system loses momentum. Leadership loses control.

An intelligent system needs leadership that can balance the urgency of visible progress with the discipline to build something that holds. The leadership that holds this line doesn't just build AI capacity. They build something competitors can't easily copy.

The Five Essentials:

1. **Policy Before Productivity:** Before anyone touches an AI tool, set explicit rules. A hard prohibition on entering financials, customer data, or trade secrets into public AI platforms isn't paranoia, it's survival.

2. **Enterprise-Grade Tools:** AI tools must offer enterprise controls: data privacy, logging transparency, user governance, and training opt-out capabilities. Free or consumer-grade versions are not acceptable where sensitive information is at stake.

3. **Input Hygiene**: Systematically scrub PII (personally Identifiable Information), sensitive terms, and proprietary client references before any AI interaction. This isn't optional. It's the last line of defense against turning AI into a data leak machine.

4. **Secure Experimentation:** Safe exploration requires controlled sandboxes with private instances, managed access, audit trails, and redacted datasets. Let people experiment but keep the guardrails up.

5. **Organization-Wide Education:** AI governance only scales when cross-functional teams understand the risks. Stop saying "deep learning" unless it matters. Use plain speak, "reduces error," "speeds response," or "requires less manual review."

What Good Looks Like in Practice

Mature companies don't just have policies, they have systems:

- They record the use and rationale for AI.
- They keep model registries and track data sources.
- They run periodic tests for fairness, accuracy, and drift.
- They include AI risk in enterprise risk frameworks.
- They train legal and compliance teams in AI governance.

If this sounds like overkill, it's not. It's the minimum needed to avoid becoming a cautionary tale in someone else's risk management presentation.

Tech debt can be refinanced. Governance debt gets called at closing. When buyers realize your AI strategy is hope and public APIs, valuation tanks.

Operator's Log

> *"We thought weekly leadership updates were enough. They weren't. Without clear governance and a single decision owner, our system build drifted. We automated the easy, visible work and ignored the foundational build. When we realized what was happening, we had already fragmented the system. It took us over a year to rebuild the sequence and regain control. Leadership cadence matters, but decision discipline keeps the system alive."*
>
> \- Portfolio Company CEO

Chapter 7

THE OLD STRATEGY v THE NEW SYSTEMS MODEL

Why Outdated Strategies Can't Survive Intelligent Systems

There's a dangerous comfort zone forming in how businesses adopt AI. It looks like progress. It sounds like innovation. But is it?

We know there's a race on. Who can move faster, automate more, and ship AI-enhanced features sooner? But speed isn't the problem, rigidity is. When a system can't change direction, moving faster just gets you to the wrong destination sooner.

That's where AI adoption often goes sideways. It speeds up systems that weren't built to adapt. It automates processes that were never designed to evolve. It speeds up strategies that quietly depend on slow, manual decision-making to stay on track.

It can look like modernizing. It can sound like a competitive advantage. But really, it's the same system, moving faster in the same direction, with the same risks baked in. That's the illusion of AI progress.

Cost-cutting and feature-chasing might feel like momentum, but they rarely build defensibility. You cannot shrink your way to market leadership.

Most strategies are built to execute, not to evolve. They assume the market will hold still long enough to finish the plan. They assume customer needs will stay inside the box drawn for them.

The Old Strategy Model

The annual strategy meeting is a relic in a world of real-time data and collapsing competitive cycles. The old strategy model followed a comfortable sequence: set a strategic direction, lock in customer problems, decide what to build, push the roadmap forward, and revisit it in 12 months. It worked when systems crawled, customers moved slowly, and competitors needed years to catch up.

But in an AI-driven market? That model quietly sets you up to lose.

When businesses build AI products using the old strategy model, they're still front-loading the work. They still assume customer problems are predictable, that market needs will hold still, and that building smarter features will protect the edge. It won't.

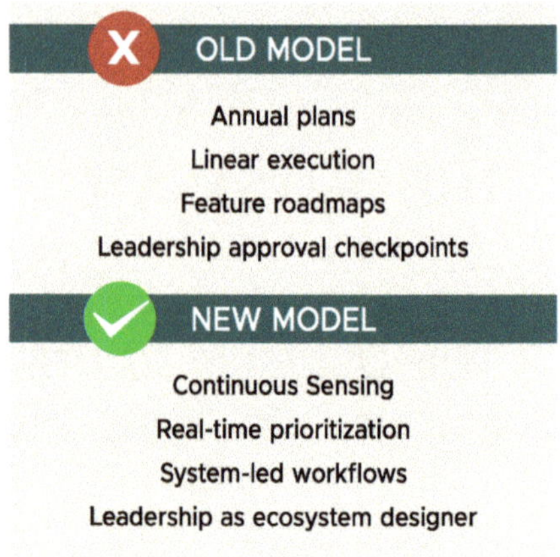

AI-powered products that solve today's problems get copied tomorrow. That feature that took six months to build? A competitor ships it in six weeks. That "smart" capability just launched? There's already an API for it.

The old model traps the business in a static race: build, launch, repeat. Each launch buys a lead, but the market outruns the roadmap. By the time the celebration starts, the feature's already a commodity.

The Strategy Shift That Matters

An AI product creates a short-term edge. An AI core creates a moving edge.

The AI core isn't a feature. It's the operating system inside the business that senses customer signals in real time, re-prioritizes problems as they emerge, and dynamically reshapes the product experience without waiting for leadership to intervene.

The AI core continuously rewrites the playbook. It drives the system to learn, adapt, and deliver new value as the market moves.

Don't just build a roadmap. Build a system that rewrites it.

In the old model, strategy asks: What should we build next? In the new model, strategy asks: What can the system sense, decide, and deliver that our competitors haven't seen yet?

The Competitive Trap

Businesses that stick to the old model will:

- Build AI-powered features.
- Launch them to market fanfare.
- Watch competitors ship the same feature months later.

- Lose the edge while they're still operating the original plan.

Worse, they're spending money to create temporary advantages in markets where everyone is solving the same problems. They invest heavily to move faster, but the advantage only lasts until the next company catches up. They're buying speed for a crowded race-course and the finish line keeps moving.

That investment might speed things up, but it doesn't make the business harder to follow. Competitors can match. Tools can replicate. APIs can flatten the edge overnight.

When AI becomes a cost sink, the spend fuels smarter features that soon belong to everyone. When AI becomes a core advantage, it builds a system that keeps tilting the game in one direction.

Mini-case: When a feature race meets a system shift (Chegg vs. ChatGPT)

Chegg was the incumbent for paid homework help. In May 2023, its CEO told investors that surging student interest in ChatGPT was hitting new-customer growth, and Chegg suspended its full-year outlook. The stock fell about 47 percent in a day.

Chegg responded with CheggMate, a GPT-4 powered learning companion. It was a fast, visible feature upgrade, but the center of gravity had already moved. A general, low-friction assistant changed student behavior at the system level, free, instant, good enough answers, which collapsed the paid funnel Chegg relied on.

Where is Chegg now? (August 2025): revenue and subscribers continue to decline, the company cut about 22 percent of its workforce in May 2025, and it sued Google over AI Overviews it says diverted traffic. Chegg is pivoting toward a "skills focused" model, investing in language learning and workplace upskilling. Q1 2025 revenue fell about 30 percent year over year to $121 million with subscribers down 31 percent. Q2 2025 revenue was about $105 million, down roughly 36 percent year over year.

Why this matters here: Chegg did not lose because it moved slowly. It optimized an old operating model while the market's system rewrote itself in real time. Features can be copied. A core that senses, decides, and adapts in motion is harder to chase. If your plan is to bolt on AI, expect the finish line to move faster than your roadmap.

Businesses that build with an AI core will:

- Build a system that adapts product behavior in motion.

- Deliver customer experiences that evolve continuously.
- Move faster than competitors can copy.
- Win by changing faster than the market can respond.

AI products get copied. AI cores keep moving.

The Strategy Rewrite

The real question isn't how fast you can build AI features. It's whether you can build a system that changes faster than your competitors can.

The roadmap is no longer just a list of features to build. It becomes a blueprint for:

- How the system should sense customer behavior in real time.
- How the system should decide which problems matter most.
- How the system should adapt workflows, pricing, or product experiences without waiting for the next quarterly planning cycle.

When a strategy starts with system behaviors instead of feature lists, everything changes.

The product stops being the differentiator. The system becomes the differentiator.

And competitors? They can't just copy features. They would have to rebuild the entire system architecture, and by the time they do, you've already evolved.

This is the edge: not what you built, but how fast you can build what's next.

Why This Matters?

The window to build this advantage is open, but shrinking.

- Companies chasing AI features will hit a wall. The speed will feel impressive, but their system will always wait for leadership to tell it what to do next.
- Companies building AI cores will move ahead. Their systems will continuously learn, re-prioritize, and deliver new value without waiting for permission.

- The companies that win will not be the ones with the best AI features. They will be the ones with the best AI cores, because that's where agility, adaptability, and defensibility live.

When you build an AI product, you build a lead. When you build an AI core, you build a moving lead that gets harder to catch.

That's the real game now.

But knowing the right strategy isn't enough. How businesses actually adopt AI, the sequence they follow, the decisions they make, and the systems they build, will decide whether they unlock a durable advantage or get trapped in the illusion of progress. Before you can build a core that moves, you have to understand the sequence that builds it.

Chapter 8

AMAZON CORE-FIRST AI USE CASE

Lessons From Native AI

Building an AI-native business is not a theoretical exercise. The world's most successful organizations have already demonstrated how embedding AI into the core operating system, rather than layering it onto legacy processes, creates sustainable, defensible value. This chapter examines an example: Amazon, the archetype of AI-powered commerce and logistics. This use case explores how a core-first approach to AI transforms business models, drives competitive advantage, and delivers results that are difficult to replicate.

Amazon: The AI Operating System for Commerce

The Challenge

As Amazon scaled from online bookseller to global commerce and cloud leader, it faced operational complexity, razor-thin margins, and relentless competition. Incremental automation would not suffice. Amazon needed a system that could sense, decide, and adapt in real time, across millions of SKUs (stock keeping units), warehouses, and customer touchpoints.

The Core-First Approach

Amazon's AI transformation goes beyond isolated features. It embeds intelligence into the company's DNA:

- **Supply Chain & Logistics:** AI algorithms dynamically route inventory, predict demand, and optimize delivery routes, enabling Amazon to offer same-day and next-day shipping at scale.
- **Dynamic Pricing:** Real-time AI models adjust prices based on competitor moves, inventory levels, and customer behavior, maximizing revenue while maintaining price competitiveness.
- **Personalization:** AI powers the recommendation engine, tailoring product suggestions, search results, and marketing communications to individual users, driving both conversion

and loyalty.

- **Fraud Detection & Risk:** Machine learning models continuously monitor transactions for anomalies, reducing fraud losses and improving customer trust.

Outcomes

- **Agility:** Amazon can respond to market shifts, supply chain disruptions, and customer trends in real time.
- **Customer Experience:** Personalization and speed have become core differentiators, making Amazon's platform "stickier" and more defensible.
- **Operating Leverage:** AI-driven automation allows Amazon to scale operations and offerings without proportional increases in cost or complexity.

Key Lessons

- **AI as Infrastructure:** At Amazon, AI is not a bolt-on; it is the backbone of the business, enabling every function to operate smarter and faster.
- **Continuous Learning:** The system improves with every transaction, delivery, and customer interaction, compounding Amazon's advantage over time.
- **Cultural Discipline:** Leadership insists on data-driven decision-making, experimentation, and relentless optimization, all supported by the AI core.

DIMENSION	AMAZON
AI Role	Operating system for commerce/logistics
Core Capabilities	Supply chain, pricing, personalization, fraud/risk
Outcomes	Real-time agility; customer loyalty; operating scale
Defensibility	Compounding system-level intelligence
Leadership	Data-driven, experimentation-focused culture

Conclusion: The Core-First Imperative

Amazon demonstrates that sustainable AI advantage comes not from isolated pilots or feature-chasing, but from building intelligence into the core of the business. Their success is rooted in:

- **System-level integration** - AI as the backbone, not the accessory.
- **Leadership discipline** - Commitment to sequencing, governance, and continuous learning.
- **Defensible differentiation** - Capabilities that competitors cannot easily copy or catch up to.

For private equity-backed companies and operators, the lesson is clear: the path to premium value and resilience lies in building an AI-native core not in chasing the latest tool, but in designing a system that learns, adapts, and compounds advantage over time.

Chapter 9

THE AI ADOPTION SEQUENCE

If the system is the advantage, the sequence builds it

Most AI adoption plans chase rapid returns, cut costs, and build features before building system intelligence. They automate the wrong processes, optimize the wrong workflows, and create a fragile system that can't adapt.

The right sequence safeguards the transformation and creates a durable advantage.

There are four phases:

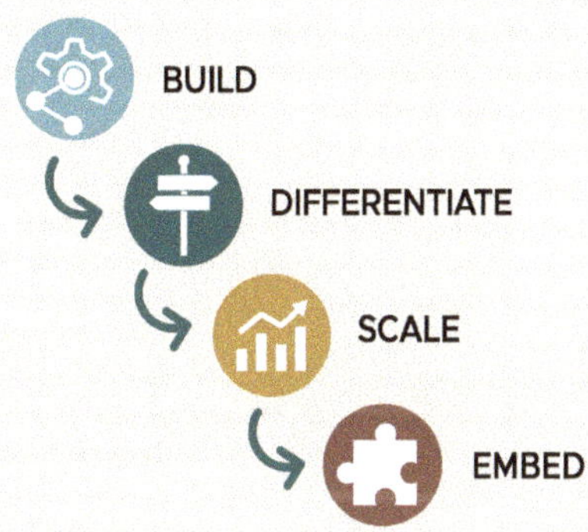

Build: Start building intelligent ability, the infrastructure that enables customer-facing workflows that drive growth and defensibility.

Use emerging capabilities to create short-term gains, i.e., generative AI, to create and automate marketing campaigns.

Differentiate: With intelligent foundations in place, create differentiated experiences, products, and workflows that competitors can't easily copy. That customers will pay more for, that plugs churn, and that broadens the market. This is the key enterprise value driver.

Scale: With differentiation working, scale intelligent capabilities across the business. Continuously improving supporting processes like finance, HR, and procurement, not just to chase efficiency, but to expand adaptability, resilience, and system-wide advantage.

Embed: Make intelligent operations part of how the business runs. Embed system-led governance, leadership cadence, and decision rights into daily workflows to sustain adaptability and prevent drifting back to old habits. This system creates a lasting advantage.

Collapsing this sequence is a common failure. Companies automate the back office first, call it a win, and lose the chance to build a real advantage. Building the right system in the right order creates a competitive distance. We will discuss how businesses choose to build, buy, or blend the capabilities needed to support this approach later, during the growth phase.

The sequence reduces execution risk, shields the growth engine, and delivers near-term results while strengthening long-term defensibility.

Starting with intelligent capabilities gives the business the foundation it needs to scale, differentiate, and adapt. This is the work that the next buyer will pay for. It's what makes the system difficult to copy and what allows the business to operate faster than competitors without sacrificing quality.

Immediate financial returns provide the momentum investors often expect, but they must not become the focus. They deliver early gains in efficiency and automation, but they are not the source of competitive advantage. This structure works because it separates the work that drives growth from the work that creates operational speed and cost savings.

It shelters the core build while showing visible progress to boards and private equity owners. It reduces the most common execution risks.

- When businesses chase cost savings first, they improve workflows that should no longer exist. They lock in old processes. They erode the ability needed to build an intelligent system later.

- When businesses start with disconnected features instead of system behaviors, they deliver fragmented solutions that do not scale, do not adapt, and do not defend the market position. Work feels busy, but it does not compound value.

- When businesses do not communicate clearly, they face internal resistance that slows delivery, undermines adoption, and blocks system-led decision-making when it's most needed.

This sequenced approach works because it avoids these traps:

- By starting with intelligence, the system gains the ability to sense, decide, adapt, and learn in real time. This enables scalable growth.

- By showing a positive impact on important metrics in parallel, the business satisfies investor expectations without derailing the core transformation.

- By delaying structural cost leverage (in secondary systems) until the core is stable, the business secures its ability to scale efficiently without damaging the growth engine.

The team moves at speed with confidence. They build a system that works differently. They build customer experiences that evolve continuously, workflows that re-prioritize in real time, and decision models that learn without waiting for the next leadership review.

The business gains adaptability, resilience, and defensibility, all qualities that make it more valuable to the next buyer.

But there is one constraint that is often overlooked. One that moves quietly but shapes everything. The leader.

The system can only move as fast as the leader allows. It can only adapt as far as the leader trusts. It can only scale as much as the leader lets go.

The next step is not about fixing the system. It is about examining the leaders who will either unlock it, or quietly throttle it.

Chapter 10

THE LEADERSHIP MINDSET SHIFT

Leaders Who Can't Let Go Will Be the Bottleneck

Building AI-native systems is not just a technology challenge. It is a leadership challenge. AI-native systems do not wait for leadership to approve the next step. They do not pause for steering committees. They do not stand by for permission to move.

An AI-native business automatically senses, decides, and adapts while it runs. It operates at system speed, not leadership speed. This shift forces a change in how leaders must lead.

Leadership is traditionally about decision control. Leaders guide daily work, approve the next step, and position themselves at the center of authority. In an AI-native business, this approach creates friction inside systems that are designed for flow.

Within a native AI organization, the role of leadership changes. The work moves from directing activity to designing guardrails that allow the system to move independently. It shifts from approving decisions to enabling the system to make them safely. The leader does not drive every outcome. The leader builds the conditions where outcomes happen without delay.

The most dangerous constraint in this shift is not the technology, the data, or the processes. It is ego.

Ego is the system killer. It shows up when a leader needs to be involved in every important decision. It appears when a leader cannot tolerate system-led moves that happen without their knowledge. It surfaces when the thought creeps in, what if the system runs better without me?

When ego is driving, leaders override system decisions to prove their relevance. They insert themselves into workflows because they feel safer when the work passes through them. They slow system decisions to make sure they are still the final word.

An ego-driven leader will slow the system by choice or by habit. They will sabotage the speed they claim to want. The system will quietly stop learning because it cannot move fast enough to capture real-time feedback. It will start to wait for leadership approval. It will shrink its own authority until it matches the leader's comfort level.

This happens not because leaders are malicious. It happens because the ego is hard to let go of.

The leader who cannot step back will always pull the system back to their pace.

In an AI-native business, leadership style is no longer just a cultural factor. It becomes an operational infrastructure. If the leadership style cannot support distributed decision-making, real-time adjustments, and system-led workflows, the company will stall. No technology stack can outrun a leadership bottleneck.

There are patterns to watch. Certain leadership styles are more likely to become a constraint.

- The dictator leader demands personal approval for every key decision. They measure importance by proximity to them. They create bottlenecks because they want to remain the center of gravity.

- The rescuer leader steps in at the first sign of system failure. They struggle to trust automated decisions. They erode system authority by insisting on manual overrides to protect the outcome.

- The hero leader trusts instinct more than system intelligence. They believe their judgment is faster and more reliable than system signals. They often bypass system feedback and rely on gut decisions.

- The prestige builder wants visible, personal wins. They invest in showcase features instead of building system strength. The core system build often gets neglected.

- The legacy operator has spent years in command-and-control environments. They rely on tight supervision and direct control. They find it difficult to trust a system that moves without waiting for their sign-off.

COMMON LEADERSHIP ARCHETYPES THAT THROTTLE AL SYSTEMS

THE DICTATOR:
Everything flows through them or doesn't move at all.

THE RESCUER:
Distrusts automation, intervenes early.

THE HERO:
Relies on instinct, ignores system signals.

THE PRESTIGE BUILDER:
Wants wins that look good, not systems that hold.

THE LEGACY OPERATOR:
Needs control, resists decentralization.

If the system waits for leadership, it's not autonomous, it's ornamental.

Each of these leaders will eventually throttle the system they build. Each will leave value on the table because they cannot step back.

The Ego Mitigation Playbook – Summary

Spotting the ego pattern is only half the work. The other half is knowing how to defuse it before it throttles your AI-native transformation.

We've built a detailed **Ego Mitigation Playbook** for each leader type, complete with step-by-step interventions you can apply pre-deal or in the first 100 days.
You can download the full version at: **www.theaifix.online**

Below are the core moves for each type:

- **Dictator:** Shift decision rights into the system and reinforce with board backing.
- **Rescuer:** Limit manual overrides to pre-agreed thresholds and document every one.
- **Hero:** Run side-by-side system vs. gut comparisons, building trust.

- **Prestige Builder:** Tie prestige and recognition to delivering core system milestones, not just visible features.
- **Legacy Operator:** Expand system-led decisions in stages to build comfort and confidence.

Leadership ego does not show up on system diagrams. It does not appear in process maps or dashboards. It appears in slow approvals, in manual escalations, and in decisions that are quietly pulled back into the leader's hands.

The leaders who succeed will design decision guardrails instead of approval checkpoints. They will trust real-time system visibility instead of requiring proximity. They will build standards into the system instead of managing exceptions themselves. They will accept that sometimes the system will make a wrong decision, and they will resist the urge to clamp down when it happens.

These leaders will build speed that the system can keep. They will build momentum that does not shrink when leadership steps out of the room. They will understand that trust in the system is a leadership skill, not a leadership risk.

This is the leadership mindset shift. The hard part is not learning the technology. The hard part is letting go of the need to control it.

When leaders let go, the system moves faster. When they cannot, the system waits.

And the future will not wait.

Leadership Style as an Investment Risk

Investors assess leadership capability in a traditional diligence process. The diligence team looks at track records, domain experience, and chemistry with the board. These are important, but they are rarely treated as structural risks to system performance.

That must change.

In an AI-native business, leadership style becomes a critical factor in whether the system will thrive or quietly collapse. The way leaders show up, their comfort with distributed decision-making, their ability to let the system run, and their willingness to trust machine-led workflows now shape the entire outcome.

Leadership style is now an operational constraint. When assessing a company:

- You are not just assessing AI readiness.
- You are not just assessing system design.
- You are not just assessing governance.

You are assessing whether the leadership can get out of the way.

If the answer is no, it is a red flag, no matter how modern the tech stack looks. This is a deal issue. This is a value creation issue. This is a readiness issue. If the leadership style is not compatible with AI-native operations, you are buying a system that is already constrained.

Smart investors will start treating leadership style as a structural risk, not a side note.

AI-native businesses can only move as fast as the leaders let them. The leadership mindset is not a footnote in this story. It is the leverage point. The system is designed to move. The leadership must let it.

Let's assume the leadership gets it. They're ready to move, to decentralize decisions, to trust the system.

Before the work begins, you need to know exactly what you're aiming toward. Many businesses confuse optimization with automation, and automation with differentiation. Let's examine the differences.

DOWNLOAD: The Ego Mitigation Playbook
This playbook equips you to spot and address leadership ego patterns that can derail AI-native transformation. It provides targeted interventions for five common leader types, Dictator, Rescuer, Hero, Prestige Builder, and Legacy Operator, along with assessment questions, governance guardrails, and 100-day action plans. Designed for use in both pre-deal diligence and post-acquisition integration, it aligns directly with the leadership readiness strategies outlined in this book.
www.theaifix.online

Chapter 11

THE THREE APPLICATIONS OF AI

Optimize, Automate, Differentiate

AI adoption often gets bundled under a single banner: "make the business better." It sounds fine in a board deck. It's also commonly where most of the thinking stops.

AI adoption has three distinct applications, and confusing them is one of the fastest ways to mis-allocate capital, build the wrong system, and end up solving the wrong problem.

The three applications are simple:

- Optimize
- Automate
- Differentiate

But they are not interchangeable, nor do they have the same strategic importance. They create different impacts. They place different demands on the system. They require different capacity plans. And they hit the financial model in different ways.

Let's separate them, cleanly , so you know exactly what you're chasing.

Optimize: Help People Move Faster in Their Work

Optimization is about creating speed for overworked people. It's AI as a co-pilot, helping humans execute faster, smoother, and with less friction. The work still needs people. The system still relies on human review, human judgment, and human hands to complete the process.

Example:

Generative AI that drafts marketing content, summarizes support tickets, or produces starter code in software development.

Optimization usually delivers fast, visible wins. It buys time; it releases pressure, and it creates breathing room for teams that are already stretched thin.

But it's not automation. It's acceleration.

When to aim for optimization:

- When resources are overworked.
- When bottlenecks come from manual work piling up.
- When the goal is to move faster without changing the underlying system.

Automate: Remove the Load Entirely

Automation is about pulling humans out of processes.

Agentic AI or agents take over entire workflows, start to finish, with minimal human intervention. This is where intelligent agents step in, decide, and push the work forward without waiting for someone to review, approve, or hit send.

Example:

AI agents handling customer renewals, triaging inbound service tickets, or adjusting prices inside pre-approved guardrails.

Automation can relieve huge amounts of operational pressure, but it's not without risk. Automating unstable processes, or automating before the system is ready, can lock in the wrong behaviors and quietly weaken the foundation.

When to aim for automation:

- When resources are overworked.
- When the process is stable, repeatable, and well-governed.
- When the goal is to remove the load, not just move it faster.

Differentiate: Build What Competitors Can't Easily Copy

Differentiation changes the game.

Differentiation is intelligent systems that shape customer experiences, product behaviors, and decision flows that competitors can't easily replicate.

This isn't speeding up or saving time. This is building system-led advantages that stretch the valuation multiple and defend the business from commoditization.

Example:

A system that dynamically adjusts pricing in real time based on live customer signals. A product that reshapes onboarding, support, and feature recommendations as the customer interacts with it.

Differentiation consumes capacity. It doesn't release pressure; it creates additional pressure.

It pulls in your sharpest people, your scarce resources, and your best thinking. It forces the system to flex in ways it's not yet designed for. It demands cross-functional coordination, real-time data flow, and intelligent decision-making that most businesses aren't ready to handle at scale.

When to aim for differentiation:

- When the system can already move fast and absorb new complexity.
- When leadership is prepared to invest in building new muscles.
- When the goal is to create customer experiences and system behaviors that are hard to copy.

AGENTS VS. AGENTIC AI: WHY THE DISTINCTION MATTERS

TRADITIONAL AGENTS FOLLOW SCRIPTS. AGENTIC AI PURSUES GOALS.

AGENTS (RULE-BASED AUTOMATION)

> Execute pre-programmed workflows
> Process tasks the same way every time
> Require human intervention when
> Conditions change

Example: chatbot with scripted Responses

AGENTIC AI (GOAL-SEEKING INTELLIGENCE)

> Pursue objectives across multiple Steps
> Adapt approach based on real-time Signals
> Learn and improve from outcomes

Example: ai that researches prospects, Crafts personalized outreach, and Adjusts strategy based on responses

Why This Matters?

When these aims get mixed up, the build drifts. Businesses automate before they've stabilized. They think they're differentiating when they're just optimizing busywork. But when you understand the difference, you can:

- Predict where the impact will land (financial or people).
- Plan for the right outcomes.
- Sequence priorities with purpose.
- Build or release the right capacity at the right time.

Each application impacts the system differently. Each one demands a different plan.

When you get this right, you can lead with precision. You can anticipate pressure before it arrives. You can build a system that won't quietly buckle under the weight of your own ambition.

The sequence sets the tempo, but it's the core that gives it weight. That's where we go next.

Chapter 12

BUILDING THE CORE

The Two Parts of a Native AI Business

Becoming a native AI business has two distinct parts: the **primary system (the Core)** and the **secondary system.** Both are essential, but only one drives differentiation.

The Primary System

The primary system is the business operating system, the infrastructure that holds intelligent capabilities. It's the engine that makes real-time decisions possible, that powers dynamic workflows, and that builds the adaptability a native AI business needs. This is where the serious weight sits.

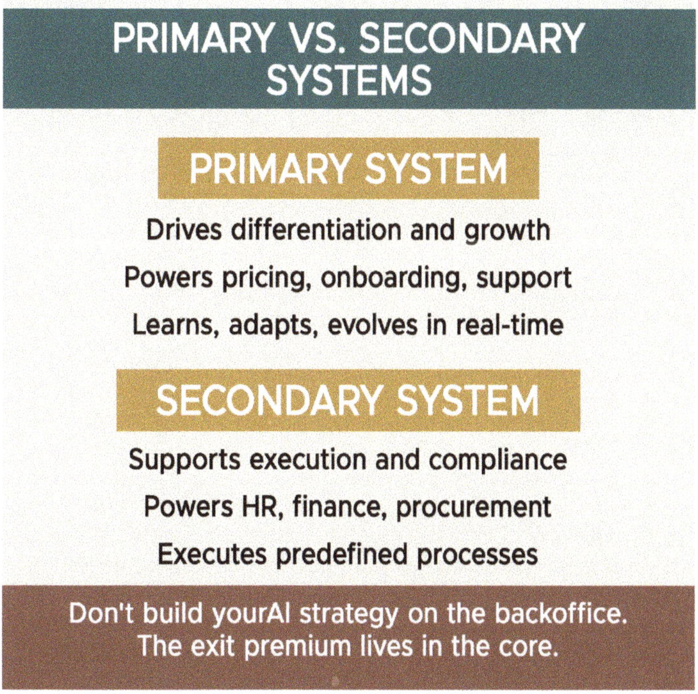

The core is the combination of workflows, data flows, and decision points that allow the business to sense, decide, and respond without waiting for human intervention. It's a system that carries pricing intelligence, onboarding logic, customer support prioritization, and product personalization. It's where the system learns in motion.

Without a strong core, AI becomes a surface feature. It can still automate tasks, but it cannot build a competitive advantage.

The strength of a native AI business comes from this system. It's the source of strategic and competitive differentiation.

With it, the business gains structural strength that is hard to copy.

The Secondary System: The Connected Business Services

The secondary system includes the critical supporting functions, HR, finance, procurement, software development, internal support, etc. These processes matter. They are the execution mechanism and the support functions that keep the business running. But they are not the source of a competitive edge.

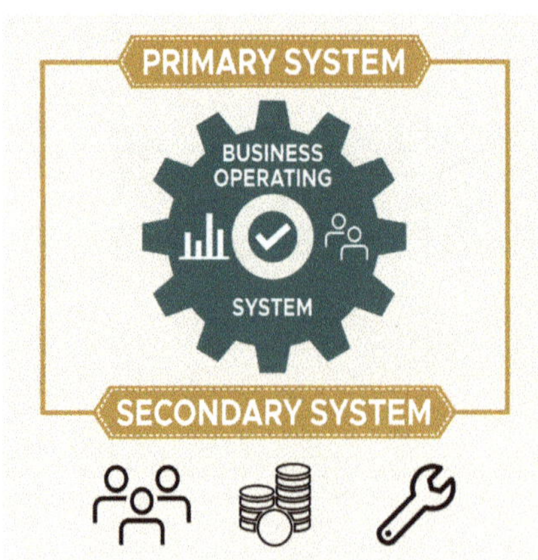

The Relationship Between the Two

The primary system sets the competitive capabilities. The secondary system supports the work. But when properly connected, the secondary system speeds up. When your supporting services can pull live data, access decision logic, and tap into intelligence-enabled workflows through APIs, they move faster and perform better. Capturing the secondary system application outputs and feeding them back to the core improves the core intelligence and its decision-making.

This is not a loose connection. It's a deliberate design. An AI-native business allows these two systems to work together in real time. When they do, the whole system compounds. When the connection breaks, the system fragments.

Building a Native AI Business

An AI-native business doesn't chase features, it builds systems that capture signals, shape decisions, and expand capabilities while in motion. These are the checkpoints that keep the system from drifting, the questions that keep strategy alive:

- Are we capturing the right signals?
- Are we shaping the right decisions?
- Are we expanding the right capabilities?

When this becomes the cadence, the business evolves as it runs. This is the design that separates tactical AI adoption from true structural advantage.

Chapter 13

SYSTEMS THINKING AND THE THEORY OF CONSTRAINTS

The Realities of Applying AI

Before becoming operators and CEOs, both authors were air traffic controllers. Every day, we made fast, high-stakes decisions in systems where the variables, plane tracks, weather, workload, and human behavior were constantly in motion. The data changed in real time; decisions could not wait, and during busy periods, decisions were delivered in an uninterrupted stream. The risks were non-negotiable. And although we didn't label it then, we were applying systems thinking and the theory of constraints in their purest form.

We didn't just move airplanes; we managed interdependencies, predicted bottlenecks, and optimized for flow under pressure. Those same principles are as critical in business, especially when applying AI. Because AI works in a system. And systems, left unmanaged, fail the moment one part moves faster than the rest.

Why Systems Thinking Matters More Than Ever?

AI is seductive in its promise, automation, acceleration, and intelligence at scale. But deploying AI without understanding the system it enters is like upgrading one engine on a multi-engine plane and ignoring the rest. Speed increases, but so does the risk of imbalance, strain, or failure.

Without systems thinking, companies miss the fact that intelligent systems behave differently. They move, they shift, they create new constraints as they run. Traditional improvement methods, focused on local efficiency, stable processes, and fixed workflows, cannot keep up.

It's more than just workflow acceleration. What changes is the shape of the system itself.

In the new world, the systems must:

- Shift priorities without waiting.
- Adjust workflows based on real-time signals.
- Sense when the constraint moves, not just when the process

slows down.

- Balance flows across teams, functions, and technology without locking in rigid steps.

This is where systems thinking shifts to design. The focus moves beyond improving the system in place and toward creating systems that can evolve while in motion.

How Systems Thinking Shapes Intelligent Systems

Systems thinking provides the blueprint for building flexibility. It changes what operators look for, what they measure, and what they build.

Map how work flows, but design for adaptability:

Follow the work across teams and functions, but focus on how those workflows can flex, not just how they can move faster.

Track where decisions get made but design them to move:

Decision points need to travel with the work. Static approvals and fixed gates will not keep up.

Build live feedback loops into the system:

Systems that cannot see what is happening in real time will miss the constraint when it shifts.

This isn't process tuning. This is building something that refuses to sit still.

Where the Theory of Constraints (ToC) Fits

The Theory of Constraints (ToC) says every system has a single limiting factor, the constraint, that caps its output. Improve anything else and you just make work pile up faster at the bottleneck. Fix the constraint and the whole system moves. Think of it as operations with a spotlight and a backbone.

ToC is not just for chasing bottlenecks. In intelligent systems, it becomes a design principle.

In traditional systems, the constraint often stays put until something big changes. In intelligent systems, the constraint moves as the system adjusts.

Designing for this means:

- Building workflows that can flex when the constraint shifts.
- Creating processes that do not collapse when capacity tightens somewhere else.
- Designing decision flows that can re-prioritize work midstream.
- Avoiding hard-coded steps that assume the constraint is fixed.

The system tracks where the constraint is today, not where it used to be.

When businesses build with the Theory of Constraints in mind, they create systems that chase the constraint, not systems that get stuck waiting for someone to notice the backlog.

How to Build It

Map the system's flow, but question where flexibility is missing: Speed without flexibility is a waste of effort.

Design decision points should follow the workflow: Don't statically align decisions to a role or process. The system incorporates decision thresholds. If a live pricing algorithm detects a market shift, the system automatically adjusts, or the decision authority moves to the team managing that pricing in the moment.

Embed live feedback loops that show where the system is slowing down now: Without real-time visibility, the system will quietly pile up problems out of sight.

Build workflows that can re-prioritize: Don't force work through the same path when the system's capacity changes, e.g., the workflow continuously checks system capacity (agent availability, ticket backlog, customer service level agreements) and re-prioritizes in real time. If capacity drops (e.g., agents are unavailable, or the system is under heavy load), the system automatically flags and routes high-impact tickets (VIP customers, regulatory issues) to the front.

Assess how the system reacts when the constraint moves: If the workflow cannot adjust, the system will fail under pressure.

Signals the System is Stuck

- Faster task completion that does not improve overall flow

- AI tools that add dashboards but never adjust workflows
- Teams that hit their local targets but push work into another backlog
- Priorities that stay fixed even when the real constraint has moved

Why This Matters?

Systems thinking shapes what works in the new world. It makes flexibility part of the build.

ToC is not something applied after the system is running. It's part of how you design the system to survive change.

If the system cannot see the constraint move, it will scale the wrong work.

AI reshapes the operating model, decision-making processes, workflows, and outcome measurement. But it only works if it fits into a coherent system.

Applying AI without a systems thinking perspective leads to isolated wins but overall chaos. When applied with a deep understanding of the system, every deployment becomes a building block for compounding improvement.

In practical terms:

- Don't start with the AI use case. Start with the system map.
- Don't chase automation. Chase flow.
- Don't assume AI removes complexity. It often just moves it.

AI Isn't Magic—It's Amplification

AI doesn't solve systemic problems. It amplifies what's already there, good or bad. That's why systems thinking is non-negotiable. If AI is to speed up value creation, start by understanding the flow of value itself.

Before launching the next pilot, ask the hard questions: Where's the constraint? What happens downstream? What breaks if this works? If those answers aren't clear, the work isn't ready. Deploying AI without asking these questions isn't strategy, it's a guess. Leading with systems intelligence turns experimentation into advantage. That's where the edge lives.

Understanding systems thinking forces you to look beyond the surface. The system is rarely broken in the places where the symptoms appear. The real constraints live upstream, in the design, in the flows, in the approvals, in the behaviors that people stop questioning.

Before you chase the deal, you need to know what you're really buying. The foundation work isn't just theoretical prep, it's what separates deal winners from value destroyers. Now it's time to move from principles to practice. In the pre-deal phase, strategy meets scrutiny. This is where assumptions get tested, AI claims get unmasked, and you find out if the business can support the kind of system you're trying to build, or if it's quietly held together with duct tape and dashboards. The groundwork is done. Now the diligence begins.

THE PRE-DEAL

Newthistle Consulting LLC

Chapter 14

OPERATOR'S FOREWORD

Seeing beyond the surface and rethinking AI in the pre-deal phase, and particularly due diligence, is now so vitally important, both for underpinning the investment thesis, but more so for unlocking premium multiple valuations at the end of the investment period.

We all know and support that diligence is the discipline that underpins every investment. It's where conviction surfaces, risk is priced, upsides are sized, and plans developed. But in the software landscape, where Artificial Intelligence is becoming a fundamental driver of competitive advantage, we are still asking some of the wrong questions, at times, not asking them at all.

Often, investors, or their advisors, treat AI as a mere formality during Technical Due Diligence. Does the company have proprietary data? Are they using ChatGPT for marketing content? Is there "machine learning" mention buried somewhere in the product roadmap? These superficial signals may provide comfort, but they reveal very little about a company's true AI readiness or future defensibility in a market being reshaped by intelligent automation, real-time analytics, and predictive capabilities.

AI is not an accessory feature; it's becoming a core element of modern tech-enabled architecture and differentiation. Not probing the depth, scalability or maturity of an AI investment strategy, AI roadmap or demonstrable case studies during diligence is not only a missed opportunity, but a major risk. Investors can and should rethink their approach to AI in technical Due Diligence.

If there is a limited or no tech due diligence (often seen in low-tech enabled businesses), what is the AI roadmap for cognitive AI application in the broader business sense: Go to Market, customer success and data/management reporting capabilities? This diligence and questioning stage can start with high-level, simple questions to originate conversations and deeper analysis:

- What does AI maturity look like in business, beyond buzzwords and basic pilot projects?

- Is there a board-approved AI strategy and operational planning document?
- What resources are allocated to AI? What costs are in the P&L?
- How do we evaluate a company's data infrastructure, because AI starts with clean, accessible, and meaningful data?
- What evidence is there in the competitive landscape of AI application? Are we good, better or best? Or just worse!
- Does the team have the talent and mindset to scale AI efforts responsibly?
- Do we know enough to assess the company's AI use cases today, and their roadmap for integrating AI in ways that drive real business value? Is this applicable not only in Tech, but throughout the entire business?
- If AI-maturity is weak, what are the competitive risks of falling behind in AI adoption, and the growth upside of getting it right?
- Are we prepared to ring-fence investment for AI advancement and maturity?

Where I see the difference in those impressive 4-5x return investments in 3 to 4 years is where investors will go deeper and faster. AI transcends mere risk management. It becomes a lever to unlock exponential value creation. But that journey starts with asking better, deeper, harder questions, earlier, and armed with that information, for better or worse, at this stage of the process, we can now help and start the planning process. Why, so when we hit the 100-day plan, we can speed up, or at least 'catch-up' and get going from day one.

Mark Rogerson – MBE MA MBA

Chapter 15

DEAL SOURCING & THESIS DEVELOPMENT

How Private Equity Firms Can Use AI for Research Advantage

"Waiting until the data room opens to learn means showing up late to the real work. By then, it's not strategy, it's scramble."

Private equity has long relied on networks, industry intuition, and banker relationships to surface deals. But those days are fading. In a market flooded with noise and inflated AI claims, the smartest firms are using AI not just to evaluate companies, but to find better ones, faster.

PE firms are still manually building lists and drowning in banker decks, but a few are using AI to surface signals from market noise, scan patents, and job posts for early indicators, and score potential targets against their thesis before the competition even knows they exist.

The New PE Research Stack

- AI models surfacing signal from market noise
- NLP (Natural Language Processing) scanning of patents, job posts, blogs, and forums
- Predictive lead scoring for targets aligned to the thesis
- Automated teardown of a company's true technical depth

AI isn't replacing instincts, it's multiplying them. The best operators now spend less time building lists and more time interrogating the right ones.

Where AI Creates an Advantage

Market Mapping That Works:

Instead of hiring expensive consultants to map subsegments, use NLP to scan industry blogs, Reddit discussions, and Crunchbase activity. Find the hidden growth pockets before they hit the mainstream radar.

Competitor Analysis at Scale:

Machine learning (ML) cluster analysis of web presence, pricing pages, and go-to-market (GTM) activity reveals which companies are genuinely innovating versus which ones are just copying the market leader. Spot the mis-priced or lagging competitors while there's still time to move.

Signal Detection That Matters:

Monitor hiring trends, product launches, and funding moves to surface emerging targets before bankers get involved. The best deals are off-market. You need to know where to look.

Tech Stack Intelligence:

Crawl job boards, GitHub activity, and Stack Overflow to understand what's actually under the hood. Separate modern, scalable architectures from legacy systems held together with duct tape and prayer.

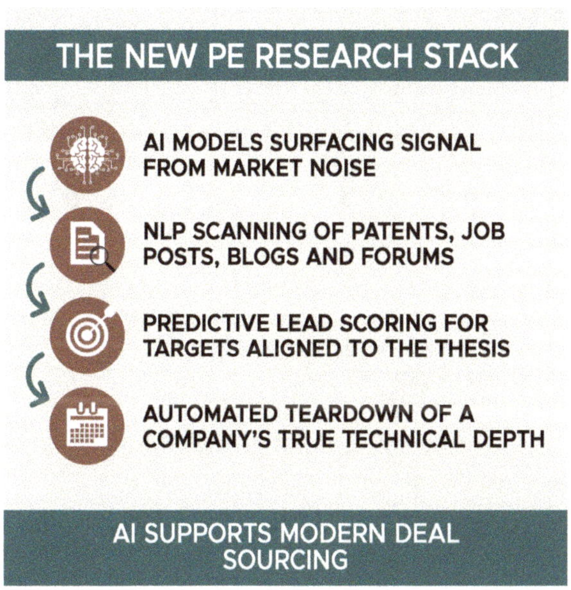

Use Cases – Blackstone and Invictus: AI in Action

Blackstone has long been treated as the lighthouse of private equity. Its embrace of artificial intelligence, however, began in a rather unorthodox setting, on a stalled bus in China. Stephen Schwarzman, seated next to Jack Ma, received an impromptu tutorial on AI. "I had no idea what he was talking about," Schwarzman later admitted, "so he gave me a quick lesson" (Institutional Investor, 2023). That chance encounter crystallized a conviction: AI was not a sideshow, but a force that would rewire the way private equity operated.

Building the Muscle at Scale

Since then, Blackstone has embedded more than 50 dedicated data scientists directly into its investment teams, far more than most of its peers. These specialists aren't in a lab on the sidelines; they work alongside dealmakers, using predictive and generative AI to sharpen sourcing, accelerate diligence, and track portfolio performance across 230+ companies (Blackstone, 2024a; Institutional Investor, 2023).

The firm has doubled down with infrastructure investments. It provided $2.3 billion in debt financing to CoreWeave, a leading GPU-rich cloud provider, to expand capacity for AI workloads. And in 2024, through its QTS subsidiary, Blackstone announced a £10 billion (~$13.3 billion) AI data center in Blyth, UK, expected to create 4,000 jobs and fund £110 million in local skills and infrastructure (Institutional Investor, 2023; Reuters, 2024).

Portfolio Impact

The results are measurable. Blackstone reported over $200 million in bottom-line impact delivered through AI-driven efficiencies across its portfolio. It has also created a 300-member advanced analytics community to circulate best practices, embedding AI know-how into more than 70 portfolio companies (Blackstone, 2024a; Blackstone, 2024b).

The lesson? At the top end of the market, AI is the connective tissue binding deal sourcing, due diligence, portfolio oversight, and risk management. Rivals can copy features; they cannot easily replicate an AI-infused culture and operating system.

Mini-Case – Invictus Growth Partners: AI at Mid-Market Scale

Of course, most firms do not have billions to throw at data centers or the luxury of dozens of in-house data scientists. Yet AI is not the preserve of mega-funds. Invictus Growth Partners, a San Mateo-based private equity firm managing mid-market enterprise software deals, built its own in-house AI engine, named Diane (Wall Street Journal, 2025).

On the sourcing side, Diane applies natural language processing and machine learning to scan job postings, patent filings, and online activity, surfacing potential deals well before bankers shop them around. This approach led Invictus to identify ThreatModeler, a cybersecurity platform, ahead of the market.

After acquisition, Diane shifts into operational intelligence, forecasting churn, detecting working-capital anomalies tied up in slow receivables and excess inventory, and flagging risks before P&L reports react. In one instance, it called out a $6 million working-capital drain three months early, freeing cash for strategic growth.

The cost? Less than $250,000 in the first year for tools and talent. The return? A multiple uplift in exit readiness and a repeatable model for future deals. For Invictus, AI is not about scale but about conviction: a proprietary edge that compounds without requiring Blackstone's billions.

Why This Matters if You're Not Blackstone

This book is not written for the Blackstones of the world. They have the resources, headcount, and patience to build global AI operating systems. Most lower mid-market firms don't.

But that is exactly the opportunity.

- Market mapping with NLP doesn't require an internal AI lab. Off-the-shelf tools can do it.
- Competitor analysis with clustering can be achieved with open-source libraries and affordable SaaS.
- Deal sourcing through weak signals can be automated from LinkedIn, Crunchbase, and job-posting feeds.
- Portfolio oversight can begin with AI-powered dashboards plugged into ERP and CRM data, no £10 billion data center required.

The edge isn't in the budget, it's in the conviction to apply AI where it compounds value: sourcing, diligence, and operational insight. The mega-funds demonstrate what's possible at scale. Firms like Invictus show it's already achievable at mid-market scale. The rest comes down to mindset.

Two Models, One Lesson

Blackstone shows what happens when AI becomes infrastructure: billions invested, 50+ data scientists integrated, and an operating system spanning hundreds of companies. Invictus shows what happens when AI becomes a focused edge: less than $250,000 invested, one proprietary platform, and a repeatable model for mid-market deals.

Both approaches work, because both are grounded in the same principle: AI compounds value when it is woven into the investment process, not added as an afterthought.

Why This Matters Now?

AI creates an advantage when applied before the auction begins. It surfaces hidden gems, filters noise, and enables pattern recognition at scale. In private equity, conviction drives capital deployment. AI gives deal teams early insights that sharpen the thesis and reduce risk. All this before the term sheet is even drafted.

Don't wait for the teaser. Let AI reveal the genuine opportunity.

Finding the right deal is just the start. Sourcing uncovers opportunities, but securing the right investment requires sharper tools. This is where the work shifts from chasing signals to testing what's real. Pre-deal due diligence is where stories crack, where surface-level AI claims face deeper scrutiny, and where discipline separates winners from wasted effort.

DOWNLOAD: AI Pre-Deal Intelligence Checklist
This checklist provides a structured approach for sourcing and evaluating deals using AI-powered market intelligence. It helps identify early signals, track emerging competitors, and assess deal potential with a system-first mindset, aligning perfectly with the pre-deal diagnostics in this book.
www.theaifix.online

References

Blackstone (2024a) Accelerating value with AI.

https://www.blackstone.com/insights/article/accelerating-value-with-ai

Blackstone (2024b) Investing in AI.

https://www.blackstone.com/investing-in-ai

Institutional Investor (2023) How Blackstone sprinted ahead of its peers in AI.

https://www.institutionalinvestor.com/article/2c5n7hypxbs38zj9xsutc/portfolio/how-blackstone-sprinted-ahead-of-its-peers-in-ai

PE Hub (2023) Blackstone is building tools to intelligently augment investment processes, says CTO John Stecher.

https://www.pehub.com/blackstone-is-building-tools-to-intelligently-augment-investment-processes-says-cto-john-stecher

Reuters (2024) Blackstone confirms £13 bln investment in Britain AI data centre.

https://www.reuters.com/technology/artificial-intelligence/blackstone-confirms-13-bln-investment-britain-ai-data-centre-2024-09-25

Wall Street Journal (2025) Growth investor Invictus banks $574 million.

https://www.wsj.com/articles/growth-investor-invictus-banks-574-million-a12c0913

Wall Street Journal (2024) AI bull Blackstone charges into data centers.

https://www.wsj.com/articles/ai-bull-blackstone-charges-into-data-centers-5033786a

Chapter 16

DUE DILIGENCE

Using AI to Uncover What Matters

Anyone who's spent a late night in a virtual data room knows the pain. Thousands of documents vying for attention, version control nightmares, and the sinking feeling that the smoking gun is hiding in a folder you'll never find.

The problem? Traditional data room review is manual, siloed, and slow. Legal, finance, tech, and commercial teams dig through their own folders, flag risks independently, and attempt to piece it all together before time runs out. By the time findings converge, it's often too late to change direction.

How AI Changes the Game

AI doesn't just speed up data room diligence, it redefines it. Instead of an archaeological dig through endless folders, AI equips deal teams with precision tools that turn chaos into clarity:

- **Ask real questions, get real answers, fast.**
  Skip the keyword scavenger hunt. With natural language querying, AI understands context and nuance. Ask, "What are the change-of-control clauses across all vendor contracts?" and get a precise, sourced answer in seconds, not a 400-page PDF to slog through.

- **Summarize complex documents in a flash.**
  AI-powered summarization distills dense legalese, technical specs, or financials into digestible briefs. No more marathon review sessions just to understand the basics. Now, a junior analyst can get senior-level clarity in minutes.

- **Spot the red flags you didn't know to look for.**
  Anomalies and inconsistencies don't hide well from machine attention. Whether it's mismatched terms, suspicious financial line items, or quietly amended clauses, AI can flag what human reviewers often miss, before they become deal-breakers.

- **Unify insights across silos.**
  Legal sees one story. Finance sees another. Ops has a third. AI cuts across departments, connecting patterns and surfacing insights that no single team could stitch together alone. It's the difference between knowing what's in the documents and knowing what it *means*.

- **Make time an asset, not an enemy.**
  Traditional reviews race the clock. AI resets it. You don't just move faster, you think faster, decide faster, and pivot earlier. That means fewer late-night scrambles, and more daylight between you and bad surprises.

What This Looks Like in Practice

Legal Teams

Can flag hundreds of non-standard clauses across thousands of contracts, detect IP ownership inconsistencies, and summarize key terms without reading every page.

Finance Teams

Can spot unusual margin trends, validate revenue recognition practices, and forecast cash flow based on historical patterns, while the legal team is still opening files.

Commercial Teams

Can assess customer concentration risk, evaluate pipeline quality, and map expansion opportunities using integrated data from multiple sources.

Technical Teams

Can review tech stack documentation, assess codebase quality, and separate real AI capabilities from marketing theater.

The Real Win: Cross-Functional Intelligence

Instead of reviewing findings in isolation, AI enables joint analysis of shared insights.

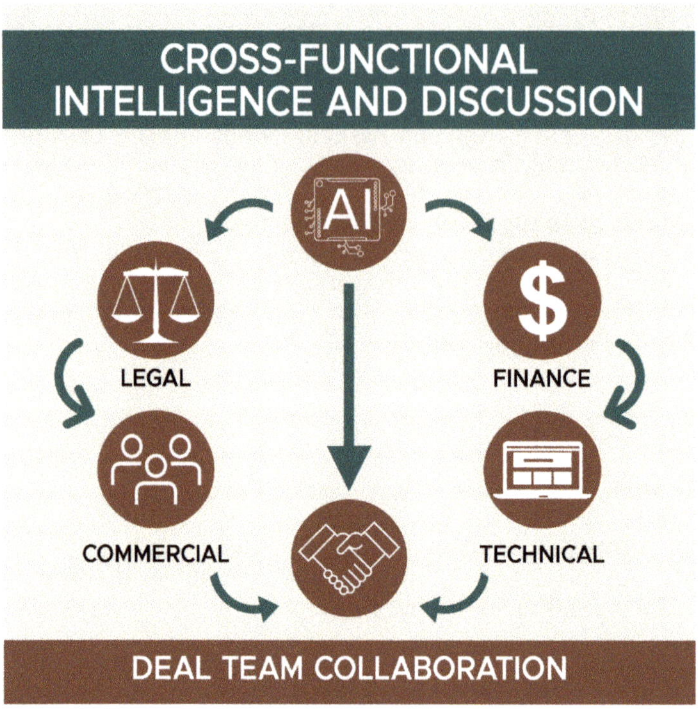

When legal, finance, and technical leads see the same flagged issues simultaneously, conversations become more productive. Risks get challenged earlier, assumptions get tested across functions, and patterns that siloed reviews miss, emerge.

A Word of Caution

AI won't replace judgment; it amplifies it. The technology is only as good as the questions you ask and the context you provide. Always verify high-stakes insights with subject matter experts. Use AI for pattern detection and summarization, not nuanced legal interpretation or strategic decision-making.

And remember garbage in, garbage out. If the data room is a mess of scanned PDFs and poorly organized files, AI can't work miracles. But it can help you see the gaps faster.

The Competitive Edge

Private equity firms using AI-enhanced due diligence are achieving remarkable efficiency gains, with reported increases of 50% in deal evaluation capacity and 90% reductions in financial modeling time (Brainforge, 2025).

Due diligence may uncover opportunity, but it doesn't guarantee readiness. Many businesses survive the surface inspection only to collapse under the weight of what comes next. Before an AI strategy can move forward, the target company's real capabilities must be tested. Assessing digital maturity is where you find out whether the business is ready to scale, or whether it's quietly built on sand.

Chapter 17

ASSESSING DIGITAL MATURITY

Why AI Starts with Digital Readiness?

If a business isn't digital, it's not ready for AI.

AI doesn't replace digital transformation; it builds on it. Drop AI into a messy, manual organization and you won't get magic. You'll get automated chaos that's worse than standing still.

That's why assessing digital maturity belongs at the very start of AI due diligence. Getting this wrong doesn't just delay value creation, it derails it entirely.

The Four Pillars of AI Readiness

Systems and Data Architecture:

AI needs structured, accessible, and connected data pipelines. If systems are fragmented or held together with manual processes, AI will starve of the fuel it needs to function.

Red flags: Data trapped in functional silos, manual data entry still required for core processes, no real-time data flows between critical systems.

Green flags: API-enabled data architecture, automated ETL (Extract, Transform, Load) pipelines, real-time integration between CRM, ERP, and operational systems.

Process Digitalization:

What isn't documented can't be automated. If workflows still depend on tribal knowledge and email handoffs, AI has nothing to optimize.

Red flags: Quote-to-cash processes that look different every time, customer onboarding that requires manual intervention in multiple steps, and approval workflows that bypass the system.

Green flags: Standardized, repeatable processes with clear handoffs, digital audit trails for key workflows, minimal manual intervention required.

Data Readiness and Governance:

Bad data doesn't just produce weak models; it produces confident decisions built on faulty foundations. The risk isn't a lack of information; it's misinformation that looks reliable.

Red flags: Customer churn calculated five different ways across teams, missing or inconsistent data in core systems, and no clear data ownership or quality standards.

Green flags: Consistent metric definitions across functions, clean master-data with clear lineage, documented data governance with quality monitoring.

Digital Behavior and Adoption:

Technology deployed isn't the same as technology adopted. If teams are still working around the system with spreadsheets and phone calls, AI will only widen the gap.

Red flags: Low system utilization rates, "shadow" spreadsheets maintained outside official systems, manual processes that duplicate system functionality.

Green flags: High user adoption of existing digital tools, data-driven decision making embedded in culture, and minimal workarounds or manual overrides.

The Cost of Digital Immaturity

When evaluating AI claims during diligence, don't overlook the hidden cost of digital gaps. A company claiming AI capabilities but lacking digital infrastructure carries more risk than opportunity.

The investment needed to retrofit digital maturity, system upgrades, process re-engineering, data cleanup, and change management erodes the expected AI upside. Worse, those AI claims may be vaporware.

Without a digital foundation, every AI promise comes with a steep discount.

What Good Looks Like

Digitally mature companies have modern systems and modern behaviors. Teams trust data over intuition. Processes adapt based on system feedback. Decisions flow through digital workflows, not around them.

These organizations can deploy AI more easily because the foundation already exists. They can scale AI safely because the infrastructure can handle it. Most importantly, they can prove AI value because they can measure it.

Digital maturity tells you what the business can do today. Leadership literacy tells you whether the business can go any further. AI-enabled growth depends on leaders who understand how intelligent systems behave, how to manage them, and how to hold the line under pressure. Evaluating AI literacy is where you find out whether the leadership team can carry the system, or whether they'll quietly hold it back.

DOWNLOAD: Digital Maturity Assessment Scorecard
This scorecard evaluates a company's readiness to adopt AI, focusing on systems architecture, process digitization, data governance, and cultural alignment. It surfaces gaps that often derail AI initiatives before they start.
www.theaifix.online

Chapter 18

EVALUATING AI LITERACY IN LEADERSHIP

Why the Right Mindset Is the First Filter?

Traditional AI due diligence processes focus on AI tools and technical assets. They assess the tech stack, data quality, and vendor relationships. But do they assess the most critical factor; can the leadership team lead through AI-driven change?

No matter how much AI potential a business has, it won't materialize if executives lack the mindset, vocabulary, or judgment to guide the transformation. Without leadership-level fluency, AI becomes a graveyard of pilot projects that never scale.

What AI Literacy Looks Like

AI literacy for executives doesn't mean coding or model architecture. It means being able to think strategically:

- Can they describe where AI fits in their business without buzzword bingo?
- Do they understand the difference between automation and intelligence?
- Have AI proposals outside strategic goals ever been rejected?
- Can they explain their data strategy without calling the CTO?

These are leadership, not technical questions. And they reveal whether AI is a strategic capability or a trophy case with nothing behind the glass.

Red Flags in the Room

Watch these warning signs during management presentations:

- CEOs who outsource every AI answer to their CTO (suggests disconnected leadership).
- CFOs who can't articulate AI's financial impact (shows missing

investment discipline).

- Operators who talk about AI like its magic (reveals superficial understanding).
- Innovation theater with no business outcomes (points to pilot purgatory).

The Questions That Matter

During diligence, ask open-ended questions that reveal thinking quality:

- How has AI changed your industry, and where do you see it going?
- Walk me through your biggest AI learning from the past year.
- What AI initiatives did you kill, and why?
- How do you measure AI success differently from other tech investments?

Listen for evidence of shared understanding across the leadership team. When different executives give conflicting answers about AI strategy, that's not just misalignment, it's execution risk.

Why This Accelerates Value Creation

When leadership already grasps AI's strategic role, the first 100 days move faster. Strategy discussions become more focused, capital gets allocated with confidence, and less time is spent explaining basics.

When that understanding is missing, part of the value creation plan must include AI literacy development. Not a deal-breaker, but a dependency that affects timing and execution complexity.

Post-Close Reality

AI fluency at the top of the org chart separates companies that scale AI from companies that struggle with it. When executives can think strategically about AI, challenge assumptions, and make confident investment decisions, everything else gets easier.

When they can't, you'll spend months building foundational understanding before you can focus on building foundational value.

A leadership team can talk the AI talk, but words don't close deals. It's time to move from assessing leadership literacy to testing whether the AI story holds up. This is where the claims meet the evidence. Validating AI claims is not a paperwork exercise. It's where the system has to prove it works, under real-world conditions, with measurable impact.

DOWNLOAD: AI C-Suite Literacy Evaluation Framework
This leadership assessment gauges whether executives are equipped to make intelligent AI decisions. It helps uncover capability gaps that can weaken governance, delay adoption, and expose the business to AI risk.
www.theaifix.online

Chapter 19

VALIDATING AI CLAIMS

Separating Substance from Vapor

"We're an AI-driven company" is the new "we're a technology company," a claim so broad it's meaningless. During diligence, the actual work is separating genuine AI capabilities from expensive automation with effective marketing.

The problem isn't that companies lie about AI, most believe their own stories. The problem is weeding out the ones who don't understand the difference between cosmetic AI and system-level intelligence.

The Three Levels of AI (And What They Mean)

Cosmetic AI: The Theater:

Chatbots, UI tricks, and timesaving widgets that rely on off-the-shelf AI look impressive, but don't connect to anything meaningful. The question isn't whether they work, it's whether they matter.

Examples: Customer service chatbots that manage 10% of inquiries, AI-generated content that still requires human editing, and recommendation engines that nobody uses.

Diligence test: "What happens to your business if this AI feature disappears tomorrow?" If the answer is "not much," you're looking at cosmetic AI.

Infrastructure AI, The Engine Room:

Embedded analytics, decision support, and data processing that could support intelligent workflows, if they're being used for decision-making instead of gathering dust.

Examples: Predictive models that inform pricing decisions, automated risk scoring that shapes underwriting, and demand forecasting that drives inventory management.

Diligence test: "Show me three business decisions made differently because of this AI system." If they can't, it's an infrastructure without impact.

Strategic AI, The System:

AI that's wired into core business operations, making real-time decisions that affect customer experience, pricing, or operations. When this layer is real, it creates defensibility. When it's faked, it falls apart under diligence pressure.

Examples: Dynamic pricing that responds to market conditions, personalized product experiences that adapt in real time, and automated workflow routing that optimizes resource allocation.

Diligence test: "How does this AI create a competitive advantage that's difficult to replicate?" If the answer is vague or generic, you're looking at wishful thinking.

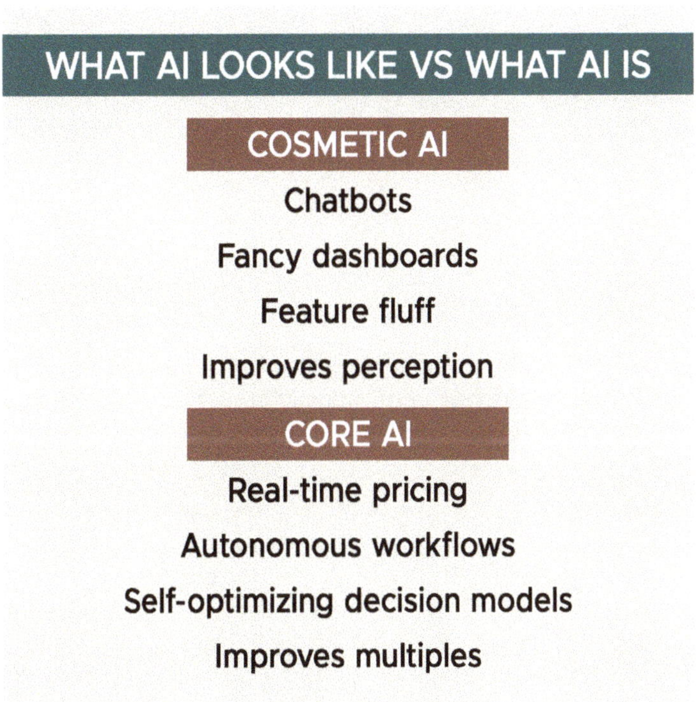

Pressure-Testing the Claims

Shadow the Use Case: Don't just ask what the AI does, walk through it. See how it's embedded in daily workflows. Who uses it? How often? With what results? If the demo requires special setup or perfect conditions, it's not as robust as claimed.

Interview Beyond the CTO: Talk to operators, finance leads, and customer-facing teams. Do they understand what the AI is doing and how it affects their work? If it's genuinely embedded, everyone should have a story about how it changed their day-to-day experience.

Audit the Value Trail: For every AI initiative, ask what changed. Which metric improved? What decision became more accurate? If there's no clear operational or financial impact, it's not value creation, it's technology tourism.

Ask About Failures: A team that has never shut down an AI project either hasn't pushed hard enough or is hiding something. Look for evidence of disciplined decision-making and course correction.

Why This Matters?

Validating AI claims isn't being skeptical for its own sake; it's understanding what you're buying. Cosmetic AI might impress customers temporarily, but it won't create a lasting competitive advantage. Infrastructure AI can provide operational benefits, but only if it's being used for decision-making.

Strategic AI is what drives multiples at exit. But it's also the rarest and hardest to fake. Companies worth backing aren't the ones with the most AI features; they're the ones with AI that change how the business operates, competes, and creates value.

The pre-deal phase is where conviction gets built or shattered. In a world where every software company claims to be "AI-powered," the ability to separate signals from noise isn't just useful, it's essential to preserving returns and identifying genuine opportunities.

Validation is where the story gets tested. The first 100 days are when the work gets real. Surviving diligence doesn't guarantee success; it just earns the right to move forward. This is where assumptions meet execution, where leadership focus matters most, and where intelligent capacity must take shape fast. The first 100 days set the tone. Get this right, and you build the system that holds. Get it wrong, and the cracks will show before the ink is dry.

DOWNLOAD: AI Capability & Maturity Worksheet
This worksheet provides a systematic framework for evaluating whether a target company's artificial intelligence capabilities are real, defensible, and valuable, or simply marketing rhetoric. With "AI-powered" claims proliferating across every industry, investors need a rigorous method to separate substance from hype before making investment decisions.

DOWNLOAD: AI Talent Risk Diagnostic
This diagnostic helps investors and operators assess the risks tied to AI-related talent within a target company. It's designed to surface gaps, dependencies, and exposure that could compromise the ability to execute or scale AI initiatives.

DOWNLOAD: AI Governance Health Scan Checklist
This checklist helps evaluate whether an AI implementation is mature, secure, and defensible. It's designed to flag governance gaps that could jeopardize valuation, expose legal risk, or fail scrutiny during diligence.

www.theaifix.online

THE FIRST 100 DAYS

Newthistle Consulting LLC

Chapter 20

OPERATOR"S FOREWORD

As an 'Operator', I have trouble with the First 100 Days. I see people 'obsessing' with the minutiae whilst the big issues get pushed. Often, the 100-day-plan lacks depth, prioritization, and practicality. At a time when the management team is generally 'burned out' from one of the most intense work experiences of their careers, 'the deal', we hit them hard on lots of little things. I must admit to some of this; I love my plan on a page. And those things 'are' important, but are they the most important?

Laying the groundwork for AI-Driven Value Creation is what is important. If we miss 2, 3, or possibly 4 quarters before we address the strategic levers for our equity story, then life is going to be much harder.

The first 100 days after the deal close are sacred. It is the window where the tone is set for the investment journey. Where focus is sharp and momentum is high. It is when investors and leadership teams align on value creation plans, assess what could work better, and agree on the things that are just not working. It is here where the real work of transformation begins.

In software businesses, particularly those under private equity ownership, the mandate for speed and scale is generally clear. But as AI becomes a foundational driver of value, the first 100 days take on new complexity, if new opportunity is not to be missed. This is not about standing up dashboards or launching a marketing automation workflow. It is about embedding the conditions for AI to truly take root, technically, operationally, and culturally.

The biggest mistake I see, especially in the earlier stage (lower-mid-market assets) is treating AI like a long-range science project or, worse, a sideshow. Too many businesses delay thinking seriously about AI until 'year two and three', mainly because there are many other fires to fight or until we feel the growth engine stalling. But by then, it is often too late to move fast enough to gain meaningful differentiation. In contrast, leading firms are using the early days post-close to get AI on the agenda, not as a project, but as a strategic pillar of value creation.

So, Day 1, where is the AI strategy group with a Board sponsor who already has executive powers of budget flexibility, a transformation fund? One of my most explosive value creation journeys was with a UK-lower-mid-market fund, which handed the management of 'off-P&L' transformation fund day one. Are we then thinking about how our AI capability and maturity become a true driver of growth, efficiency, and defensibility?

AI in private equity-backed software companies cannot be a 'maybe'. It now must be a matter of when and how well. The companies that move decisively in the first 100 days, building AI fluency, identifying strategic use cases, ring-fencing internal and external resources, and investing in capability are the ones that will create enduring value and outpace their peers. What you do now in these first 100 days will set the course for what is possible later. The AI journey begins on day one. It begins now.

I have watched more businesses than I can count stumble into the first 100 days. The ink is barely dry on the deal, and suddenly everyone is sprinting to put points on the board. The pressure is real, get a win, show momentum. This is where the trapdoor usually opens.

The first 100 days are famous for where value is won or lost, but: it's where discipline can often fall apart. The scrambling begins. A flurry of disconnected AI pilots, a chatbot here, an automation over there, a nice dashboard. It looks like progress, but it isn't. It's activity without systems thinking; it's movement without value.

We have all sat through those meetings. We have all seen AI presented as a sideshow, a collection of AI ideas stapled into old systems that should have been scrapped. We have seen businesses shrink their potential by automating workflows that had no business existing in the first place.

It happens because the first 100 days feel like a race, and when the clock is ticking, people naturally want to grab whatever win is closest. There is nothing wrong with this, but it's not optimal and won't be the foundation we are truly seeking.

AI is not the prize. Building the ecosystem is the prize.

The businesses that build intelligent capacity into their primary systems, customer-facing, revenue-driving, differentiation-building systems, are the ones that will create real value. They don't just look good in month three; they hold up under pressure when it's time to sell, and our buyer is looking for an ecosystem that it can leverage quickly.

This 100-Day Phase is about getting our hands around the business, doing some things faster and better, embracing due diligence findings: stabilizing revenue and stopping unnecessary cash-bleed, locking down renewals, reinforcing recurring revenue streams, shoring up cash collections, tightening commercial discipline, and fixing the operational leaks that we have identified. All super important stuff. Something generally we all do pretty well,

But, and here is the big 'but'. At the same time (not in Q2 of Q3) this is where the foundation for AI should be blueprinted, agreed/endorsed and resourced. The system is not going to be built correctly, or quickly, unless these early critical AI moves land in the first 100 days.

By the end of our 100-days we need to make sure that:

- We truly understand the health of our enterprise data. What we have, where it is and how it can be harnessed or what we need to do quickly to harness it.
- That the team that will define and build the primary AI system is identified and resourced.
- We look for ways to score easy points. Only where they create momentum without pulling resources off the primary system.
- We start building AI literacy into the operating rhythm. People can't work in an AI-native system if they don't understand it. Training, communication, and system design need to move together.
- We deploy visible, fast AI use-cases that align with the intelligent capabilities' evolution. These aren't side projects, they're proof that the system can learn and improve in real time.

Cost saving and process improvement still have a place, they always will. There's nothing wrong with delivering operational improvements, faster reporting, smoother procurement, better internal tools. But those are support acts, they're not the main event. They don't make a business defensible; they don't create pricing power; they don't get buyers fighting over the deal. If these subordinate projects start driving the story, the core system build is already in trouble.

This part of the book is about creating the optimal sequence, and making sure the work in the first 100 days survives contact with the real world.

The first 100 days aren't just a clock; they're a test. They're when businesses decide whether they're building something intelligent or just playing a faster version of the old game. Let's get it right.

Mark Rogerson – MBE MA MBA

Chapter 21

AI READINESS

Understanding Your Starting Position

The fastest way to stall an AI initiative is to drop it into an organization that isn't ready for it.

In many portfolio companies, the barrier isn't the algorithm, it's the absence of the basics. Data is scattered, systems don't talk, governance exists in name only, and the leadership team still thinks AI is an IT project.

That doesn't make AI adoption impossible. It means the first stage of the journey is about laying track before you roll out the train.

The Digital Readiness Ladder

AI readiness isn't binary. Most companies sit somewhere on a spectrum of maturity, and each rung on the ladder unlocks new capabilities, but also carries risks if you stay there too long.

Stage 1 — Foundational
Data in at least one core business area is clean and accessible, ERP or CRM is in active use, and basic reporting processes are in place.

- **Capability gained:** Ability to run standard reports, clean core data sets, and prepare systems for integration.
- **Risk of staying here:** High failure rate for AI projects; every proposal is a one-off experiment with no repeatable process.
- **Board move:** Approve a targeted audit of one critical business function's data.
- **Management move:** Clean and integrate those priority data sets; document reporting processes.
- **Capability build:** Deploy basic reporting tools; train teams on data entry accuracy.

Stage 2 — Enabled
A governance framework exists and is applied, executives understand the difference between automation and intelligence, and decision rights for technology adoption are clear.

- **Capability gained:** Ability to launch AI pilots with clear oversight and decision-making processes.
- **Risk of staying here:** AI remains stuck in silos; missed opportunities for cross-functional impact; limited scalability.
- **Board move:** Mandate an AI literacy sprint for the leadership team within 60 days.
- **Management move:** Enforce governance checkpoints for all AI proposals.
- **Capability build:** Develop internal AI guidelines and invest in secure data-sharing infrastructure.

Stage 3 — Adaptive
Cross-functional workflows are connected, AI is applied to live monitoring and alerts, and small-scale automation is in production.

- **Capability gained:** AI insights used in cross-functional decision-making, reducing latency in responding to risks or opportunities.
- **Risk of staying here:** Adoption becomes inconsistent, benefits plateau, and competitors with native AI integration may overtake.
- **Board move:** Require quarterly AI performance reviews tied to cross-functional KPIs.
- **Management move:** Expand AI monitoring into additional workflows; train managers to use insights in operational decisions.
- **Capability build:** Create AI feedback loops; standardize data models across departments.

Stage 4 — Native
AI is fully integrated into strategy, operations, and board decision-making. Systems and leadership evolve together, with continuous improvement and adaptation.

- **Capability gained:** AI becomes a competitive moat; decisions and strategy adapt continuously with market changes.

- **Risk of staying here:** Complacency, governance erosion, and slow response to new AI capabilities.
- **Board move:** Integrate AI impact measures into board packs and strategic planning cycles.
- **Management move:** Automate high-value processes at scale; maintain ongoing AI model updates.
- **Capability build:** Embed AI retraining cycles; develop an internal AI innovation lab.

Scoring Your Readiness

This ladder works best as a self-assessment. For each stage, rate your organization from **1 (low)** to **5 (high)** against the indicators described. Use evidence, not assumptions.

Total your score across all stages and map yourself here:

- **4–8 points: Early Stage (Foundational Focus)**
  Concentrate on cleaning and integrating data, establishing governance, and building AI literacy in leadership. Avoid major AI projects until these basics are locked in.
- **9–12 points: Building Momentum (Pilot & Enable)**
  You have the structure to run targeted pilots. Focus on high-probability, low-risk use cases that demonstrate tangible value quickly.
- **13–16 points: Competitive Edge (Scale & Integrate)**
  You're ready to embed AI across functions and into board-level decision-making. Now the priority is creating defensibility and weaving AI into your equity story.

Why Readiness Drives Value

Boards often treat readiness work as overhead, a cost with no immediate payoff. In practice, it's the opposite. Companies that invest early in clean data, functional governance, and AI-literate leadership scale faster, adapt more quickly, and hold their valuation longer than those that try to skip the build.

Readiness isn't a pause in the journey. It's the first leg of the race, the difference between burning out engines on gravel roads and leading the field when the course opens up.

Chapter 22

WHAT DOES THIS NEW SYSTEM LOOK LIKE?

From Static Packages to a Self-Learning Business OS

It's easy to talk about building intelligent systems. It's harder to see what that looks like in practice. Remember, the primary system is the core OS of a native AI business and what leads to differentiation customers can feel. Secondary systems are the execution and support functions. What does it mean to change strategy, build new differentiators, and intelligently apply AI to primary and secondary systems?

Changing Strategy: Moving From Fixed Packages to Dynamic Experiences

A traditional software company sells fixed subscription packages. Customers choose from three tiers, each with predefined features and pricing. The strategy is fixed. The roadmap assumes these fixed packages.

Imagine buying a car. Today, you buy the base model and choose fixed packages: sport, winter, technology, or luxury. Driving off the lot locks in those choices. You can't swap packages. Some companies send over-the-air feature updates, like turning on heated seats or unlocking advanced driver assist, but these are binary switches. You either have the feature, or you don't.

An intelligent system changes this. Imagine if the car packages adjusted based on how you drive. If you spend most of your time in the city, it optimizes fuel efficiency and urban handling. If you frequently drive in snow, it offers heated seats and quietly shifts to prioritize traction and cold-weather settings. If you move to Florida, the heated seats are disabled and you don't pay for the service.

The system adapts and learns from customer use. An intelligent product recommends features, upsells, and cross-sells based on how the customer uses the product and what their support history reveals about their actual needs. It reshapes the offer to fit the customer, not the other way around.

This is a strategy shift. It changes how to package value, how to sell the product, and how the business competes. It needs a system that adjusts without waiting for a quarterly roadmap update (with oversight when necessary).

Building Product Differentiators: Real-Time Customer Journeys

Customer journeys are mapped, hard-coded, and driven by pre-approved workflows in a traditional system. AI speeds up the steps, but the paths remain rigid.

In an intelligent system, the customer journey adapts.

Imagine a software product that senses when a user is about to churn. It notices the slowdown in activity, the increase in support tickets, and the hesitation on key features. Instead of waiting for a scheduled intervention, the system adjusts the customer's experience in real time.

It proactively changes onboarding, shifts product recommendations, or routes the user to higher-touch support without leadership needing to approve it first.

This is what product differentiation looks like. It's not a faster version of the old process; it's a different system behavior.

Intelligent Secondary Systems: Sales and Marketing

Sales and marketing still rely on handoffs, periodic campaign reporting, and static lead scoring models. AI is often dropped into automate email or to speed up CRM updates, but the core sales and marketing system remains manual and slow.

In an intelligent system, the sales process becomes adaptive.

Imagine a system that responds to an inquiry by first researching the business, target markets, needs, and current providers. It uses research to create a unique marketing campaign to convert that prospect into a customer. The system automatically prioritizes the lead, personalizes the next set of touchpoints, and reshapes the outreach without a sales manager to review the queue.

Marketing adjusts in real time. Campaigns evolve based on live performance signals, not batch reports. Lead scoring is no longer a fixed formula; it continuously learns which signals predict conversion.

AI is not a faster CRM update. It's a system that changes the way sales and marketing work.

The path forward is building these kinds of intelligent systems, the ones that move with the customer, adapt as they go, and learn in real time.

Chapter 23

THE BACKBONE OF AN INTELLIGENT SYSTEM

From Ambition to Architecture

An intelligent system cannot operate on ambition alone. It needs a technical foundation that allows it to sense, decide, adapt, and learn while moving. This is not a wish list of innovative technologies; it's a focused set of capabilities that must work together to build a system that moves intelligently.

The Key Layers of a Native AI Business

1. The Technology Stack

This is tarmac, tires, and fuel. Cloud infrastructure, data pipelines, observability, MLOps, GPU orchestration, zero-trust security, boring until it breaks, indispensable when speed matters. Instrument every cost here: tokens, bandwidth, GPU hours. If FinOps can't see it in real time, expect a nasty invoice surprise.

2. The Primary System (The Core)

Think of this as the operating system for an AI-native firm. It has three jobs: sense, decide, and push the decision into the workflow before a human opens Slack.

3. Artificial Intelligence

Models live here, not as temple relics but as hot-swappable parts. The orchestration layer picks the best model for the job, logs every inference, and flags drift before Twitter does. Guardrails, policy, bias, safety, run in code, not in a PDF nobody reads.

4. Continuous Learning & Real-Time Data Capture

Every action feeds new telemetry back into the Lakehouse. The system retrains, retests, and redeploys while users keep working. Your feature velocity is now limited only by GPU queue time.

5. Dynamic User Experiences

Front-end that adapts like a good waiter, anticipates needs, offers specials, refills the glass before it's empty. Multimodal concierge, intent detector, digital-twin playgrounds. Customers feel the intelligence, not the engineering.

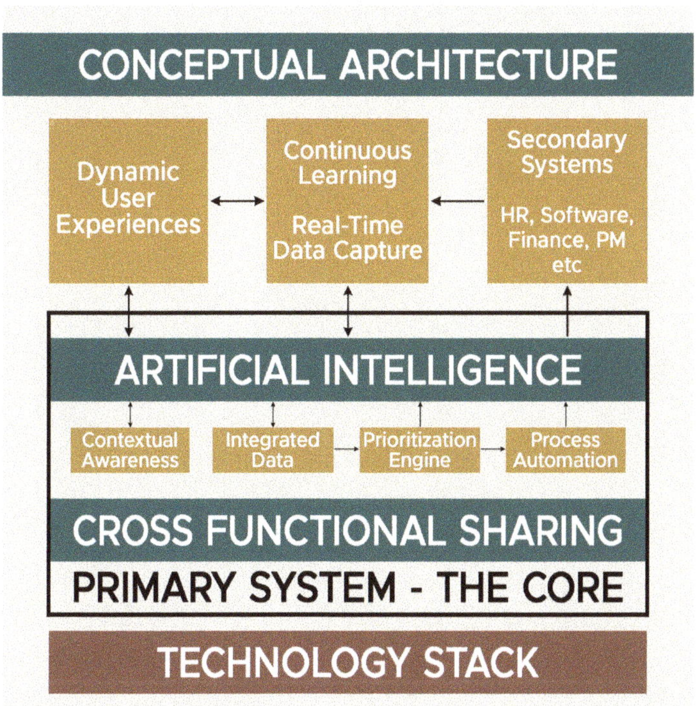

Build all five layers and every release sparks the next learning loop. Miss one and you're back to shipping static features while the market speeds past, packages fixed, strategy guessing, and system stalled.

Begin at the base. Worn tires on a Formula 1 car will slow you down or even end the race early. Skimp on data pipelines or MLOps and AI is theoretical speed.

Automate the boring, amplify the valuable. Any layer that doesn't cut latency between signal and action is décor; rip it out.

Instrument every cost. Tokens, GPUs, and vector search look cheap until usage triples. FinOps belongs in architecture diagrams, not after invoices arrive.

Guardrails beat gatekeepers. Policies live in code. Squads ship without begging for signatures. Security approves the pipeline, not each commit.

Design for swap-ability. Your edge is how fast you replace today's "best" model with tomorrow's upgrade. Treat models like brake pads, not fine art.

SUB-LAYER	WHAT IT REALLY DOES
Cross-Functional Sharing	Exposes the same live truth to sales, success, finance, and ops. No more "my spreadsheet vs your BI dashboard."
Contextual Awareness	Tags every event with whom, what, when, risk, and value so the system knows if a spike matters or can wait.
Integrated Data	Data Lakehouse, live collection, sharing.
Prioritization Engine	Ranks tasks, tickets, or product ideas continuously. Static queues die here.
Process Automation	Executes the decision, refund, reroute, rebuild model, without scheduling a meeting.

Knowing the architecture is not enough. Understanding AI is not enough. Building the technical backbone is necessary, but building is where trade-offs get real. Every business faces pressure to show immediate improvements. Designing and balancing is how leadership learns to defend the system while still moving the work forward. This is where priorities collide and discipline matters.

Chapter 24

WHAT MUST BE TRUE

The Leadership, Governance, and Capability Foundations That Hold It Together

Building an AI-native system goes beyond sequencing tasks on a roadmap. It depends on creating the conditions that allow the system to run, adjust, and grow without stalling. Without the right foundations in place, even the best-structured plan will eventually wobble.

The first 100 days set the tone. This is where the groundwork for the AI-native future is locked in or quietly compromised.

Ownership and System Accountability

Start with an AI Strategy Lead. Not a shared responsibility, not a dotted line to five people, not a committee. One person must own the system's success, hold the sequence, and keep leadership attention on the work that matters. This isn't a project manager with a fancier title. It's someone with the authority and business fluency to steer system-first decisions.

Don't chase the smartest AI technician and hand them the keys to strategy. The AI genius has his or her place; you need that person. That person is not the strategy lead.

The AI Strategy Lead needs to understand the P&L, not the Python. They need to know when to say no to a technically elegant solution that doesn't serve the business model. They must have the weight to push back on both the tech teams and the executive sponsors when the sequence is at risk.

The technical genius is essential to building and scaling models, setting up the pipelines, and ensuring the system's architecture can hold. But the strategy lead is the one who knows where the business is going, how AI fits into the investment thesis, and which system-first decisions will move enterprise value.

The two roles work together. The AI genius builds capability. The AI Strategy Lead shapes the system's role in the business and keeps the build tied to the value that buyers will pay for.

Confuse these roles, and you either end up with a brilliant system no one needs or a cost-cutting sideshow that cannot deliver. Get this right, and you build something that lasts.

Governance and Decision Authority

Lock in early AI governance. Authority and accountability must be unambiguous. Who approves when the system can re-prioritize work? Who monitors model performance? Who green lights system-led decisions? These rules prevent system fragmentation later.

Governance is not a side process. It lives inside workflows, not in a policy manual on the shelf. Oversight happens in real time, not in a quarterly review. Live monitoring, decision accuracy tracking, and intervention rules are baked into the build from Day 1.

Building the Right Team

No system builds itself; it's built by a team. Borrowed resources won't cut it. The team includes AI product managers, MLOps engineers, and data specialists who build, deploy, and monitor intelligent systems in production.

But the *who* and the *when* are not fixed. They depend on the rollout plan and the type of AI technology the business is deploying.

If the initial focus is on traditional machine learning, like predictive models, risk scoring, or demand forecasting, you'll need strong data scientists, model validation specialists, and MLOps engineers to build and maintain scalable pipelines.

If the plan leans toward generative AI applications, like natural language processing, customer-facing chat, or content automation, the team needs different strengths. You'll need prompt engineers, AI ethics reviewers, and interface designers who make the system visible, accessible, and safer for broader teams to use.

If the goal is to build agentic AI systems, those capable of goal-seeking, multi-step workflows, and real-time adjustments, you'll need AI product managers who design system autonomy and carefully balance decision guardrails. These systems require deeper cross-functional governance, which means hiring specialists who understand how to design for embedded safety and continuous oversight.

The skills you need shift with the system's maturity. Early-stage builds need system architects, API integration specialists, and data engineers to get the foundation right. As the system scales, the need shifts to model retraining, system monitoring, and governance operations that track how the system behaves under pressure.

Don't rush to build a generic AI team. Match the roles you need to the rollout sequence, the system design, and the specific AI technologies you're adopting when you need them. Build the wrong team at the wrong time, and you either stall the system or burn resources solving problems you won't face for another 12 months.

Smart sequencing applies to people, too.

Verifying System Readiness

The first 100 days are where the business pressure tests what already exists. Before building anything new, leadership needs to know whether the current systems can carry the weight of an AI-native build.

This isn't a wish list or future state diagrams. It's evaluating the systems that are in place today, how data moves, where it gets stuck, and whether the architecture supports real-time decision-making.

Start by mapping where the data lives, how it flows, and what's still trapped in functional silos. Systems that rely on batch uploads, manual handoffs, or disconnected reporting structures will choke an intelligent system before it gets off the ground.

Live data pipelines are not optional. If the system can't see what's happening, it can't think. The first 100 days must surface if continuous sensing, real-time prioritization, and system-led adjustments are possible with the current infrastructure.

Security and governance are evaluated as core system components. An AI-native system changes how data moves, who has access, and where decisions are made. If security and IT controls can't keep pace with those changes, the system will fail at scale.

The answers to these questions shape the roadmap and resource planning. They will dictate how long the drive to native AI takes, and if the system will hold when the real work starts.

Communicating the System's Purpose

If the system isn't clearly explained, people will fill in the blanks themselves, and not in your favor. Silence is dangerous. Employees will invent their own stories about AI, and those stories aren't good.

Explain the plan early and often. Include the workforce in early planning.

If AI is viewed as a cost-cutting weapon or a threat to jobs, it will fail, no matter how well it's built.

This is leadership discipline. A system that's invisible to the people using it won't hold.

Roadmap Discipline

The roadmap is where good intentions either hold or unravel. The pressure to show visible progress is relentless, but cutting corners on the roadmap is the fastest way to collapse the system.

Milestones need to track if the system is behaving as expected. A project delivered on time doesn't count if the system still can't re-prioritize or improve customer experience on the fly.

The roadmap isn't a report for the board; it's the guardrail that holds the system.

Execution Groundwork: Key Principles

Every decision in the first 100 days either contributes to or compromises. These principles maintain order:

- Intelligent capacity comes first.
- Subordinate projects in secondary systems stay in their place.
- Ownership is visible, and system-first decisions stay at the top of the agenda.
- The operating team drives the dual-track build, not scattered initiatives.
- Governance and data pipelines are used, they don't only fill the filing cabinet.
- Success hinges on system behavior, not task completion.

Closing

The first 100 days are where the foundations laid create either an advantage that compounds or a fragile system that can't scale when it matters. Protecting the system is a choice. So is drifting from it. This is the moment where leadership decides which story they're writing.

Laying the groundwork gives the business a chance to succeed. The next step is creating a roadmap that will survive the pressure, the pace, and the inevitable distractions. The roadmap must do more than sequence the work. It must hold the system together as it moves.

Chapter 25

THE 100-DAY ROADMAP THAT HOLDS

Structured Enough to Matter, Flexible Enough to Survive

The first 100 days set the path that leads somewhere. If the work isn't structured, focus is lost. Immaterial victories will pile up in the wrong places.

So a structured roadmap matters.

This roadmap isn't for a superficial slide presentation. It's there to stop the drift. It's there to keep the plan from collapsing under the pressure of the demand for immediate results.

This is a disciplined rollout. It's a roadmap for sequencing the work in a way that results in real foundational intelligence while showing simultaneous, visible progress.

But this isn't a rigid schedule. The roadmap should adapt to your business, your leadership cadence, your current AI maturity, and the speed at which your teams realistically move. Some businesses will progress faster; some will need more runway. Some will already have AI initiatives in flight, others will start from nothing.

Use this roadmap to build the structure that fits your business.

The 100-Day Plan: Stabilize & Align

This plan is structured across three phases. Each phase holds the sequence and balances the need for visible wins with the intelligent system build.

Phase 1: Day 1–30

Set the Foundations

- **Appoint the AI Strategy Lead and AI Technical Lead:** Make decision authority visible.
- **Launch the Communication Plan:** Communicate retraining, capacity management, and role changes early. Be transparent.

Be specific. No delays.

- **Audit the System's Readiness:** Assess workflows, data pipelines, and technology stacks. Confirm whether current tools can support AI ambitions or whether gaps must be closed.
- **Prioritize:** Separate primary system capability builds from secondary system efficiency and cost-savings. Lock leadership commitment to the native AI goal.
- **Plan for Surplus Capacity:** Plan early for excess capacity and how to deal with it. Identify growth initiatives that can absorb it before pressure pushes toward cuts.

Phase 2: Day 31–60

Plan the System Build

- **Define the primary system requirements:** Build intelligent capacity. Focus on live signal tracking, data gathering, and real-time decision automation.
- **Lock the Sequence:** Monitor closely for resource drift. Stop primary system progress from getting sidelined.
- **Launch Retraining Programs:** Deliver real retraining, mapped to the future system's needs.
- **Align the Technology Stack:** Finalize decisions on tooling and integration. Avoid fragmenting the stack across incompatible platforms.
- **Govern Surplus Capacity:** Track where free capacity goes. Keep it focused on growth initiatives, not quiet cuts.

Phase 3: Day 61–100

Prove Progress

- **Operationalize Primary System Wins:** Demonstrate capabilities that deliver immediate results.
- **Stand Up System Governance:** Activate live monitoring of AI-driven decisions. Assign owners to watch for system drift and unintended outcomes.
- **Track and Communicate Progress:** Provide visible updates. Show that retraining is working, surplus capacity is redeployed, and the intelligent system is evolving.

- **Reinforce Culture and Trust:** Deliver on retraining promises. Manage departures with transparency and empathy. Show the business that this is a credible, ethical system build.
- **Lock Momentum:** Prepare the next wave of intelligent system expansion. Confirm funding, resource allocation, and leadership focus for the next phase.

Summary Milestones

This is where the value starts compounding. You're about to lock in how to build real differentiation, how to grow multiples, and how to create the kind of system that competitors can't easily touch. When this lands, the system moves with purpose. This is the moment to press on, build with discipline, and shape a future that lasts.

The first 100 days have set the system in motion. What comes next in the PE deal cycle is transformation and growth. This is the phase where leadership decisions shape the system's trajectory, where intelligent capacity starts driving real business outcomes, and where value creation either compounds or collapses. Growth isn't automatic. It has to be earned. That's where we go next.

DOWNLOAD: 100-Day AI Implementation Timeline
This roadmap is designed to help operating leaders in newly acquired companies sequence AI-related activities during the critical first 100 days of ownership. It enforces disciplined sequencing, links every initiative to the investment thesis, and adjusts execution style to match leadership dynamics. The goal is to generate visible early wins without undermining governance, culture, or long-term scalability.
www.theaifix.online

GROW & SCALE

Newthistle Consulting LLC

Chapter 26

OPERATOR'S FOREWORD

Growth is under pressure; yet we know strong organic growth is not optional in our World. In today's market, every AI initiative needs to be tied to specific business outcomes: revenue expansion, improved gross margin, cash flow resilience, or cost discipline. Broad claims of "value creation" aren't enough. The bar has been raised: leaders need to show how an initiative delivers a measurable financial impact, not just momentum.

The last few years have brought seismic shifts to the global economy. Inflationary pressures, rising interest rates, and supply chain volatility. Unpredictable geopolitical events have conspired to compress margins, dampen demand, and elongate sales cycles.

Many of the traditional levers that Private Equity firms have pulled for decades, geographic expansion, pricing strategies, and sales acceleration, now yield diminishing returns or carry greater risk. Even the brightest minds in growth strategy are finding themselves in a more complex, volatile landscape.

Enter AI, not as a silver bullet, but as a powerful, underutilized tool in the modern growth arsenal which few are embracing (for now). Artificial Intelligence has the potential to do for growth what Excel once did for finance, transform workflows, uncover hidden insights, and drive smarter, faster decision-making. Automation and efficiency matter, but the real driver is intelligence. AI can help businesses see where growth is truly coming from, engage customers in new, revolutionary way, helping us to better understand what customers really want, which segments are underserved, and which behaviors correlate with churn, expansion, or cross-selling success.

The era of easy growth is over, if there ever was one; but right now its over. But with the right AI capabilities, focused in the right way, a new growth lever is emerging: smarter, faster, more predictive, and more sustainable than ever before.

Mark Rogerson, MBE MA MBA

Chapter 27

THE HARD GROWTH PATH

Building Value That Buyers Pay For

How do we create value that holds? The chapters ahead explore how to sequence growth, decide whether to build, buy, or blend key capabilities, and how to convert the work into added enterprise value.

Growth is not the headline. Native AI is the headline. Growth is just proof that the system works.

There's a familiar pattern at this stage of the PE journey. The race begins with visible customer growth and revenue acceleration. Teams start chasing whatever moves the numbers fastest. It feels like momentum until it falls apart.

We understand that the drive to integrate AI cannot interrupt these critical activities. The old ways don't stop and wait for future capabilities. The executive is still expected to deliver results.

The growth we want isn't powered by bigger budgets or flashier campaigns. It comes from systems designed to create sustainable growth and long-term value, systems that are agile, adaptable, and expandable as markets shift, customer preferences evolve, economic conditions tighten, and technology advances. When the system is built this way, growth holds under pressure. When it's rushed, growth collapses the moment the market changes or the questions get harder.

Why This Phase Is Different?

Private equity pressure doesn't ease up during the growth phase; it intensifies. The clock is still ticking, the exit story is already being shaped, and every metric gets scrutinized for sustainability. Some companies buckle under this pressure. They push for whatever moves the numbers fastest.

The companies that build durable value stay focused. They keep building intelligent capacity. They doubled down on systems that create differentiated customer experiences.

There's always an easier path; it leads to fragile growth that looks strong until someone starts digging. The hard path builds systems that buyers fight to acquire.

What Growth Looks Like with Intelligent Systems

When the system is working, growth accelerates across multiple dimensions simultaneously:

- **Revenue grows faster** because pricing adapts and offers personalization without friction.
- **Margins expand** because intelligent workflows remove bottlenecks without driving up costs.
- **Customer retention improves** because experiences shift with the customer, not just react later.
- **Net revenue retention (NRR) rises** because expansion gets triggered by live signals, not static calendars.
- **Customer acquisition cost (CAC) drops** because targeting and pipeline optimization happen in real-time.
- **Sales cycles shorten** because opportunities surface and route faster based on actual buyer behavior.

This is why the system was built, not to tick efficiency boxes, but to create compound value that stacks across every metric that matters at exit.

With the growth path now framed, the next decision is whether to build, buy, or blend the capabilities needed to scale intelligently.

Chapter 28

BUY vs BUILD vs BLEND

Choosing the Right AI Path

After completing the roadmap, the next consideration is delivery. Buy a commercial solution, build in-house, or blend both approaches? Each path carries trade-offs in speed, cost, control, and long-term adaptability.

The buy, build, or blend decision shapes more than the technology stack. It influences capital efficiency, time-to-value, and how well the solution scales with the business' needs. Get it wrong, and you'll drain runway on tools that never fit. Get it right, and you'll convert strategy into execution faster and leaner.

When to Buy (And When Not To)

In many cases, buying is the fastest and most practical approach. AI platforms and APIs have matured significantly. They're stable, scalable, and highly effective for common tasks like content summarization, support ticket classification, or lead scoring.

Buying also minimizes upfront investment. The value hypothesis assessment and move to production happen in weeks rather than quarters. Buying avoids the burden of model training or infrastructure maintenance.

But convenience comes with trade-offs. Buying, locks in vendor pricing, roadmap, and pace of innovation. In regulated industries or use cases involving sensitive data, privacy and integration concerns may outweigh the convenience factor.

The Middle Ground: Blending Tools and Customization

For nuanced use cases, especially those tied to proprietary processes or unique datasets, blending commercial tools with internal customization often strikes the right balance.

This might involve fine-tuning an open-source language model with internal support transcripts, building a RAG (retrieval augmented generation) pipeline that pulls from proprietary documentation to generate specific and relevant AI answers, or wrapping a vendor API in workflows tailored to how your business actually operates.

Blending does raise the technical bar. You need engineers or data scientists who can integrate, monitor, and evolve the solution. The benefit is greater flexibility and stronger returns on proprietary data. The trade-off is added complexity and maintenance overhead.

When to Build from Scratch (Rarely)

Custom development should be the exception, not the rule. The threshold is high: the capability must be core to your product, differentiated in the market, and impossible to achieve with off-the-shelf solutions.

Common examples include custom underwriting engines in FinTech, domain-specific intent detection in conversational platforms, and real-time decision systems in supply chain or logistics.

Building requires significant investment in talent, infrastructure, and long-term stewardship. But when justified, it creates differentiated capabilities, defensible IP, and tighter alignment with your strategic narrative at exit.

Making the Call: A Decision Framework

A few key questions can guide the decision:

- **Is this capability strategic or a commodity?** If it's non-differentiating, buy it. If it defines your product or creates a moat, consider building or blending.
- **Do you have proprietary data that materially improves performance?** Unique datasets may justify investment in customization where vendor tools fall short.
- **Can you sustain this capability internally?** Without the right people or infrastructure, managed services might be the better near-term fit.

The Growth Phase Reality Check

In the growth phase, both capital and time are limited. The objective is results, not building an inventory of tools that look good on a slide. Start lean, move fast, and earn the right to invest further.

Ambition often gets confused with complexity. Teams spin up internal builds before validating use cases or commit to bespoke systems before understanding user needs. A more disciplined path starts simple, proves value, and levels up only when the ROI is clear and defensible.

In AI, as in strategy, elegance comes from choosing the simplest effective path and knowing exactly when to scale up.

DOWNLOAD: AI Talent Strategy Framework & 100 Day Execution Playbook

This framework provides a systematic approach to AI talent strategy decisions and execution, moving beyond simple "buy vs. build" thinking to address the complex realities of AI talent acquisition, development, and retention. It integrates strategic assessment, financial modeling, risk evaluation, and detailed execution planning to ensure the right talent strategy supports business objectives.

DOWNLOAD: AI Team Readiness & Development Worksheet
Leadership AI literacy directly correlates with AI initiative success. This diagnostic scorecard evaluates the AI readiness of key leadership roles across the organization, identifying specific capability gaps and development priorities. Unlike technical assessments, this scorecard focuses on business leadership competencies necessary for guiding AI strategy, making investment decisions, and driving organizational adoption.

www.theaifix.online

Chapter 29

LESSONS FROM THE FIELD

Real-World Outcomes of the AI Buy–Build–Blend Choice

When it comes to embedding AI into a portfolio company's operating model, leadership faces a deceptively simple choice: build the capability in-house, buy it off the shelf, or blend the two. The right answer depends on urgency, capital discipline, integration complexity, and the company's appetite for defensibility. In practice, the trade-offs become clear when we examine real-world decisions.

Build – Control, Customization and Capability Development

Hewlett Packard Enterprise (HPE) offers a textbook example of the build path. In 2023, after an internal hackathon revealed the inefficiency of relying solely on external tools, HPE's legal team chose to create their own AI-powered contract drafting solution. By building internally, they avoided the licensing constraints and data governance concerns that come with vendor platforms, while tailoring the tool to their existing workflows. The upfront investment was higher, and rollout slower than a purchased alternative, but the long-term benefits included tighter integration, complete data control, and defensible IP (Wong, 2023).

Buy – Speed and Simplicity

Sometimes, the cost of waiting outweighs the benefits of custom development. Staples Canada confronted that reality when it adopted Luminance's AI-powered contract management system. Instead of spending months on design and build, Staples went live quickly, immediately improving contract turnaround times and risk review capacity. While this approach delivered value at speed and avoided the IT burden of an in-house build, it left Staples exposed to the same vendor product available to competitors, reducing defensibility over time (Wong, 2023).

Blend – The Hybrid Play

Meta Platforms, formerly Facebook, has pursued a hybrid strategy, acquiring external AI talent and infrastructure while continuing heavy internal investment. In 2025, Meta acquired a 49% stake in Scale AI, gaining access to cutting-edge data-labeling capabilities and experienced AI engineers, while simultaneously expanding its own AI research and deployment infrastructure. This accelerated development timelines and broadened its technical bench, but created integration complexity between acquired capabilities and in-house systems. If the execution is disciplined, the payoff is a highly defensible capability set; if not, the complexity risks slowing the entire initiative (Roumeliotis, 2025; Neptune.ai, 2023).

Buy-and-Build in Private Equity – Scale as Defensibility

In the PE world, blending often takes the form of a buy-and-build strategy. Summit Partners' roll-up of Infor provides a strong example, using the initial acquisition as a platform and completing nine add-on acquisitions to expand market coverage, broaden capabilities, and consolidate share. The combined scale not only improved cost leverage but also increased defensibility, as competitors would need to match the breadth of capability and customer base to compete effectively (Moonfare, 2024; Bain & Company, 2024).

Buy vs Build Vs Blend Summary Table

Strategy	Example	Cost & Speed	Integration	Defensibility
Build	HPE Legal Tools	High initial cost, slower deployment	Tight integration, full control	High (proprietary)
Buy	Staples Canada, AdoptedLuminance	Low cost, fast to deploy	Moderate (vendor-dependent)	Low (non-exclusive)
Blend	Meta + Scale AI	Very high investment, fast scale	Complex (integration challenges)	Potentially very high if aligned
Buy-and-Build	Summit → Bought Infor & add-ons	Moderate cost, strategic accumulation	Synergy-rich if managed well	High (scale & breadth)

Closing the Chapter

The buy vs build vs blend decision is more than a procurement choice, it's a strategic fork in the road that determines how fast a company can move, how tightly AI integrates into its operations, and how hard it is for competitors to copy the result. Building offers maximum control and defensibility but demands patience and capital. Buying delivers instant impact but leaves little moat. Blending, whether through partnerships, acquisitions, or add-on strategies, can produce the best of both, provided leadership is prepared to manage the integration risks. For PE operators, the decision should always be framed not just by today's need, but by the narrative you will need to sell at exit.

Intelligent growth needs more than system design; it needs financial discipline that keeps the investment focused. Without clear financial guardrails, even the smartest builds can drift into vanity projects or resource drains. Investment with financial discipline is what keeps the system aligned to value.

DOWNLOAD: Buy vs. Build vs. Blend Worksheet
This framework helps leadership teams make disciplined decisions about AI capability acquisition, balancing speed, control, cost, and strategic value while maintaining financial discipline.
www.theaifix.online

References

Bain & Company (2024) *Building a Stronger Buy-and-Build.*

https://www.bain.com/insights/building-a-stronger-buy-and-build-global-private-equity-report-2024/

Moonfare (2024) *5 Examples of Private Equity Value Creation.*

https://www.moonfare.com/blog/5-examples-pe-value-creation

Neptune.ai (2023) *Build vs Buy: How to Choose Your Machine Learning Platform.*

https://neptune.ai/blog/ml-ai-platform-build-vs-buy

Roumeliotis, G. (2025) *Meta's Buy-and-Build AI Merger Lacks Synergy.* Reuters.

https://www.reuters.com/commentary/breakingviews/metas-buy-and-build-ai-merger-lacks-synergy-2025-07-16/

Wong, J. (2023) *Law Firms Embrace AI Contract Tools but Weigh Build vs Buy.* Financial Times.

https://www.ft.com/content/b5ec2894-3628-4083-90ff-d671533c3da8

Chapter 30

INVESTMENT WITH FINANCIAL DISCIPLINE

Allocating Capital to Build Systems That Endure

Financial discipline in AI is choosing to invest in work that builds intelligent capacity, even when opportunities to reduce costs are sitting in the corner looking like an easy win.

Before approving any AI investment, ask: Does this build intelligent capacity into the system? If it doesn't, it doesn't belong in the investment plan. Every dollar should fund work that makes the system smarter, more adaptive, or more capable of scaling decisions without human intervention.

What Deserves Investment?

Intelligent Decision Systems

Back the engines that turn live signals into action. Invest here when decisions repeat at scale and latency costs money.

- Pricing models that adjust automatically based on customer signals.
- Resource allocation systems that optimize in real-time.
- Customer journey orchestration that personalizes without manual triggers.
- Predictive maintenance that prevents problems instead of reacting to them.

System Learning Infrastructure

Models without feedback go stale. Build the plumbing that captures outcomes and feeds them back so the system gets better with use.

- Data pipelines that capture decision outcomes and feed back into models.
- A/B testing frameworks that continuously optimize based on

real performance.

- Feedback loops that improve recommendations as the business scales.
- Analytics that reveal which system behaviors drive the best outcomes.

Adaptive Workflow Engineering

Smarts are wasted if work cannot move. Engineer flows that re-prioritize in context and route decisions to where they create value.

- Processes that can re-prioritize work based on changing conditions.
- Approval systems that route decisions based on context, not hierarchy.
- Customer support that escalates issues based on predicted impact.
- Supply chain systems that adjust purchasing based on demand signals.

Don’t Fund

Protect capital from distractions. The items below consume attention without strengthening the core or moving financials.

AI Tourism Projects

Curiosity belongs in a sandbox, not the capex plan. If a pilot lacks a path to production and scale, it is sightseeing.

- Experiments with no path to production or scale.
- Proof-of-concepts that solve problems nobody actually has.
- Technology showcases that impress but don't integrate.
- Pilot projects that duplicate existing functionality with marginally better performance.

Convenience Automation

Time savers that leave decision quality unchanged are local efficiencies, not value creation. If it does not improve the choice, skip it.

- Timesaving tools that don't change decision quality.

- Report generation that's faster but not more actionable.
- Workflow shortcuts that avoid system integration.
- Dashboard enhancements that look good but don't drive behavior.

Feature Theater

Pretty demos do not move valuation. If a feature cannot shift customer behavior or defensibility, it is packaging, not progress.

- AI that bolts onto products without changing core value.
- "Smart" features that customers don't use or value.
- Competitive response features that don't strengthen market position.
- Innovation for innovation's sake without a clear business impact.

The ROI Reality Check

AI investments should be judged by system impact, not project completion. The question isn't "Did we build what we planned?" It adds, "Did the system get smarter, more adaptive, or more valuable?"

Strong AI investments compound over time. Weak ones create maintenance burden without ongoing value. The difference is if the work contributes to an intelligent system or just creates more sophisticated complexity.

Managing the Investment Portfolio

Treat AI investments like a disciplined portfolio, not a scattered list of projects. Every initiative, every allocation, must map to future value. If it doesn't, it doesn't belong.

- Fund diverse bets across different value drivers, customer experience, cost leverage, market expansion, and not redundant shots at the same problem.
- Shut down initiatives that don't deliver measurable system improvement or show a clear path to sustainable growth.
- Double down on scalable wins that strengthen system adaptability or build long-term competitive advantage.

- Capture and share what didn't work. Documented failures stop future investments from repeating past mistakes.

The portfolio isn't built on perfect prediction. It's driven by evidence-backed allocation that steadily builds enterprise value.

Every dollar must connect to future value, or it's a distraction.

But disciplined investment is only half the battle. Without governance, even the smartest capital allocations can erode over time.

Chapter 31

GOVERNANCE AS VALUE PROTECTION

Why AI Without Policy Erodes Enterprise Value

As we have previously discussed, governance starts on day one. It's not a phase you get to when the system is live or when the exit is in sight. But early governance isn't enough. As the system scales, governance must continuously mature, evolve, and tighten; otherwise, the system becomes a silent liability.

The risks are real; they are operational, and they will open the company up to legal liability that will destroy valuation if left unchecked.

Where Governance Fails—And Value Gets Eroded

Legal Time Bombs

- **Data Protection Failures:** Uncontrolled AI processing can easily violate data privacy laws, often without anyone realizing it until the damage is done.
- **IP Contamination:** Models trained on unvetted datasets can introduce third-party IP, creating ownership disputes that surface in diligence or, worse, after the exit.
- **Unclear Ownership:** AI-generated content and code without documented ownership trails can trigger costly legal battles.

Security Exposure

- **Sensitive Data Leaks:** Connecting AI systems to public models without proper isolation can leak confidential information.
- **Missing Audit Trails:** When AI decisions can't be reconstructed, the system is immediately exposed to governance, security, and trust failures.
- **API Vulnerabilities:** Poorly secured AI APIs can become backdoors into core systems.

Bias and Brand Risk

- **Discriminatory Outputs:** AI systems that haven't been stress-tested for bias can trigger PR crises and legal action.
- **Lack of Fairness Testing:** Without built-in fairness protocols, AI outputs can quietly damage the brand before anyone notices.
- **Opaque Decision-Making:** Systems making decisions that leadership can't explain or defend will not survive regulatory scrutiny.

Operational Fragility

- **Single Points of Failure:** When AI expertise is concentrated in a handful of employees, turnover can quietly collapse system resilience.
- **No Documentation:** Without clear logs for model maintenance, retraining, or deployment, system stability can erode quickly.
- **Vendor Dependencies:** Relying on third-party vendors without clear service level agreements (SLAs) or transition planning creates brittle dependencies.

These aren't edge cases. These are common breakdowns that will surface in buyer diligence, and they crush deal value.

What Good Governance Looks Like

Mature companies treat AI governance like financial controls. It's not optional. It's not paperwork. It's an essential infrastructure.

The Policy Stack

- **Enforced AI Acceptable Use Policies:** Not just written, but actively monitored and enforced.
- **Model Risk Guidelines:** Documented approval workflows for every significant AI deployment.
- **Data Handling Procedures:** Defensible, auditable processes that can stand up to regulatory review.

Operational Controls

- **Deployment Approvals and Retraining Logs:** Every production model should have a visible record of who approved it, when it was last retrained, and what changes were made.

- **Cybersecurity Protocols:** AI systems must be embedded within broader security frameworks, complete with certifications, access controls, and documented safeguards.

- **Bias Testing and Explainability:** Bias assessments, fairness testing, and explainability records should exist for all critical AI models.

Human Oversight

- **Escalation Protocols:** Clear rules for when AI-driven decisions must be elevated to human review.

- **Audit Sign Offs:** Regular, independent reviews of AI system behavior and outputs.

- **Role-Based Training:** Documented AI governance training by role, proving that the leadership team knows how to govern the system they've built.

Governance Must Mature

Governance isn't static. As the system grows, as AI touches more workflows, and as new capabilities come online, the governance model must evolve. The cadence must increase. The oversight must deepen. The documentation must be hardened. Good governance moves with the system. It adapts to the build, to the growth, and to the complexity of the market.

This Matters at Exit

When buyers arrive, they will evaluate whether the governance is real or performative. They will check whether the logs match the story. They will expect escalation pathways, audit trails, and evidence that system changes were managed deliberately.

Governance is a defense mechanism. It's what shows buyers the system can be safely scaled, safely inherited, and safely relied on. Governance protects the system, the story, and the valuation.

What started as simple oversight in the first 100 days must grow into a fully mature system that can manage complexity, speed, and cross-functional decisions without breaking. Governance must move with the system. Let's discuss how.

Chapter 32

GOVERNANCE MATURITY ACROSS THE PE DEAL CYCLE

Building Governance That Scales

Governance is not a set-and-forget checklist. It's a living, expanding discipline that must grow with the system.

The risks aren't static. What feels manageable in the early build can quietly fracture the system at scale. The decision pathways that work in a small, fast-moving team will buckle when the business stretches across new markets, functions, and customers. Without governance that matures, intelligent capacity decays into system sprawl, unmanageable risk, and valuation loss.

First 100 Days: Establish

Lay the foundation, define controls, and set the initial guardrails.

Growth Phase: Expand & Embed

Scale governance, operationalize controls, and deeply integrate across the business.

Exit Preparation: Evidence & Transfer

Prove governance maturity, package documentation, and ensure seamless transferability.

The businesses that will succeed are the ones that deliberately evolve their governance as they grow. They enforce discipline while scaling. And they enter the exit process with a governance story that holds under buyer scrutiny.

Building Governance That Moves with You

Governance that worked in the first 100 days will not hold during the growth phase. And governance that holds in the growth phase will not satisfy buyers at exit. The system's maturity depends on the governance maturing alongside it.

AI Governance Maturity Framework by Growth Stage

Strong businesses don't treat governance as a defensive layer. They treat it as critical infrastructure that secures value, and scales with growth.

GOVERNANCE ELEMENT	FIRST 100 DAYS	GROWTH PHASE	EXIT PREPARATION
Leadership Ownership	Appoint AI Governance Lead with decision rights.	Expand governance leadership across functions.	Ensure buyer-facing governance roles are visible and transferable.
Decision Rights	Define who can approve model deployment and system changes.	Distribute decision rights with oversight to cross-functional teams.	Ensure clear documentation of all decision approvals and escalations.
AI Acceptable Use Policy	Create, publish, and begin enforcement.	Actively monitor compliance and refine based on operational learning.	Demonstrate enforcement history and audit logs.
Model Risk Guidelines	Establish initial approval workflows.	Expand workflows to include retraining cycles and adaptation rules.	Provide documented approval history for all critical models.
Data Handling Procedures	Build defensible, auditable data processing protocols.	Strengthen data governance with lineage tracking and access control.	Show regulatory readiness with clean data audit trails.
Bias and Explainability Controls	Start bias testing and record initial explainability practices.	Mature fairness testing, scenario 5. stress tests, and monitoring at scale.	Provide full bias testing history and explainability documentation.
Deployment and Retraining Logs	Record initial model deployments and training cycles.	Maintain detailed logs for all production models and retraining events.	Provide audit-ready retraining and change history.
Security Protocols	Embed AI systems into cybersecurity frameworks.	Maintain certifications, conduct regular security reviews.	Provide security audit logs and vendor SLA confirmations.
Escalation Protocols	Define escalation points for AI-driven decisions.	Operationalize human-in-the-loop checkpoints at scale.	Document escalation pathways and decision overrides.
Human Oversight Training	Train leadership and key users on AI governance basics.	Expand role-based AI training across the organization.	Provide complete training records and buyer-facing evidence.
Vendor Management	Map AI vendor relationships and initial SLAS.	Tighten vendor controls and establish transition contingencies.	Ensure vendor contracts, dependencies, and exit-readiness documentation are clean.

But even the best governance can only hold the system together. It cannot solve the next leadership challenge: what happens when efficiency starts pulling attention away from system strength? That's where we go next.

DOWNLOAD: Governance Development Workbook
As artificial intelligence becomes embedded in business operations, proper governance becomes essential for managing risk, ensuring compliance, and maintaining stakeholder trust. This health scan evaluates the completeness and effectiveness of an organization's AI governance framework across all critical dimensions.
www.theaifix.online

Chapter 33

THE EFFICIENCY PARADOX

When Success Creates New Problems

Some things are easier to deny than to fix. When intelligent systems work well, they create surplus capacity. And when that happens, the default corporate response is as predictable as it is destructive, cut costs.

That's exactly where businesses break their own systems. **The Problem is Human, Not Technical**

The system automates customer support workflows. Response times drop. Tickets get resolved faster. The efficiency metrics look fantastic. But the dashboard doesn't show the remaining support staff now see AI as a job threat, not a growth engine.

They stop leaning into the system. They resist new use cases. They quietly work around the technology that was supposed to move the business forward. The system slowly grinds down because the people who power it no longer trust it. This isn't a workflow problem. It's a cultural fracture.

When efficiency leads to cuts, employees don't get smarter about AI; they get smarter about protecting themselves from it. Trust breaks fast. Morale fades. The system stalls because the people driving it resist it.

The Efficiency Paradox in Action

Picture this: AI improves your finance team's productivity by 40%. Fantastic, right? Here's what happens:

Month 1: The team celebrates faster month-end closes.

Month 3: Leadership asks, "Do we really need the same headcount?"

Month 6: Two finance roles get eliminated "because of AI efficiency gains."

Month 9: The remaining team starts avoiding the AI tools.

Month 12: Productivity drops below pre-AI levels because no one trusts the system.

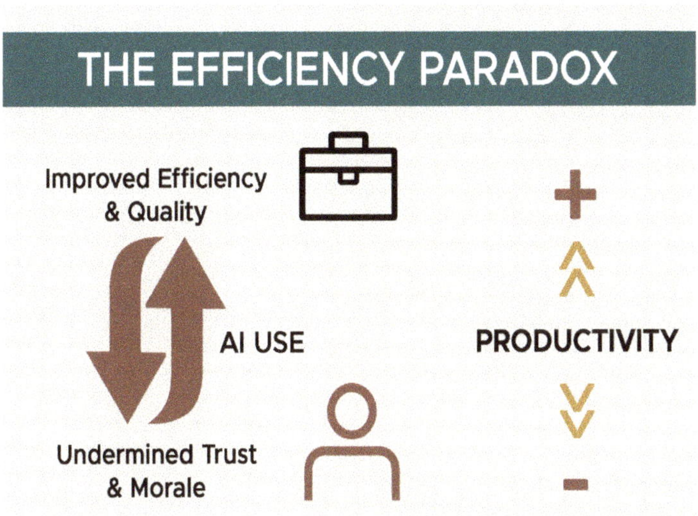

The Human Cost of Automated Efficiency: Real-World Examples

The pursuit of automated efficiency, especially in customer service, is often a classic example of the efficiency paradox. The initial gains look great on a balance sheet, but the hidden human cost can quickly turn them into a long-term liability.

A powerful example of this is the Swedish fintech company **Klarna**. In its drive to cut costs, Klarna heavily invested in AI-powered chatbots and reportedly laid off 700 employees. The company's CEO publicly boasted that their AI assistant could perform the work of 700 full-time human employees. This move, however, had unintended consequences. Customers began to complain about a decline in service quality, and the company faced public backlash. Klarna eventually had to reverse its decision, acknowledging that human interaction was still essential for handling complex issues and maintaining customer satisfaction. This case demonstrates that simply replacing people with AI, without a strategy for the remaining workforce, can lead to a disastrous drop in service quality and a damaged brand reputation.

Another example comes from the tech giant **IBM**. In an effort to streamline its human resources department, IBM introduced an AI-powered system called AskHR to handle many routine queries and administrative tasks. The automation was intended to free up HR staff for more strategic work. However, the system struggled with tasks that required empathy and subjective judgment. While it was efficient at handling simple requests, it couldn't manage complex, sensitive employee issues. IBM was eventually forced to rehire some of the HR staff it had laid off, recognizing that the AI system could not replicate the human touch necessary for many of its most critical functions.

Denham Sadler (2025) Companies backtrack after going all in on AI.

https://ia.acs.org.au/article/2025/companies-backtrack-after-going-all-in-on-ai.html

These cases highlight the core flaw in the "automate and cut" strategy. When companies prioritize short-term cost savings, they fail to see that a disengaged and fearful workforce will resist new technologies. The remaining employees, fearing for their own jobs, quietly work around the system, withhold critical feedback, and ultimately cause productivity to stall. These examples show that the efficiency paradox is not just a theoretical problem; it's a very real business risk with measurable financial and reputational consequences.

The Real Solution: Plan for Surplus Before It Arrives

You've automated your way to a worse outcome. The solution seems easy. They are now surplus. Let them go! Right?

Smart businesses approach efficiency differently. They plan for surplus capacity before it happens. They decide early where freed people will go and what growth initiatives will absorb their time.

Managing the Paradox:

- **Be Honest About Trade-Offs Upfront:** Hiding the human cost breaks trust. Being clear about where roles will change builds credibility, even when the conversation is tough.
- **Invest in Real Upskilling:** Not rebranded training sessions that lead nowhere. Actual capability-building that gives people ownership over the next round of system improvements.
- **Phase the Automation:** Rushing full automation in one wave triggers cultural rejection. Gradual deployment gives people time to find their new roles inside the system.
- **Share the Benefits:** When intelligent systems free up capacity, the gains shouldn't bypass the people who made it work. Salary increases, shorter work weeks, and meaningful bonuses. Show that efficiency serves everyone, not just the balance sheet.

Why This Matters for PE-Backed Companies?

When your eye is on exit multiples, not quarterly metrics, you can afford to invest in your people. Redeploy capacity instead of cutting it, and share the benefits without flinching.

But if you're trapped in short-term cost-cutting mode, every decision collapses into efficiency theater. The system gets faster, but the business gets weaker.

The companies that pass this test build intelligent systems that keep growing. The ones that fail build systems that stop working because the people inside them stop pushing. Those early gains soon turn to a financial liability when the transition to native AI fails prematurely.

New Roles in a Native AI Company

Retraining Must Be Real, Specific, and Offered Upfront

When intelligent systems replace manual work, some roles will disappear. But don't be another company that gets it wrong. They treat retraining like a consolation prize instead of what it is, a system requirement.

Why Retraining Can't Be an Afterthought?

In an AI-native business, the people who know the current system best are exactly the ones you need to build, run, and scale the next version. But only if you give them an actual path to get there.

A vague promise to "discuss retraining later" won't be trusted. It is seen as a delaying tactic. If retraining isn't built into the communication plan early, your workforce will assume the worst. Trust and leadership credibility will erode before the first automation is even deployed.

The New Roles (And What They Do)

When businesses go AI-native, what do these roles look like?

System Designers, Not Process Administrators: When task-based roles shrink, you need people who design intelligent workflows that adapt in real time. These aren't project managers, they're system thinkers who know how to build processes that sense, decide, and adjust without waiting for manual triggers.

AI-Centric Commercial Operators: Sales and marketing shift from relying on static playbooks to managing dynamic, constantly evolving pipelines. Real-time signal tracking, AI-driven lead prioritization, and dynamic pricing engines become standard. Someone needs to run this new machine. Who is best suited to design and manage this reality, a tech guy or the sales manager you just let go?

Live Data Interpreters: Forget monthly reports. The system moves on streaming data, live dashboards, and real-time signals. You need operators who can spot meaningful shifts as they happen and intervene when the system's decisions need human context.

Human-AI Collaboration Specialists: The handoffs between human judgment and system intelligence need to be designed, not hoped for. These roles figure out when humans step in, when they step back, and how to keep system behavior aligned with strategy.

Why Upfront Communication Matters?

If some roles won't exist in the future system, that conversation needs to happen upfront. Letting people go early, with notice, transparency, compassion, and meaningful support, shouts leadership empathy and credibility.

The alternative is worse. Signal that everyone is safe, then cut later, and you've just taught your organization that AI initiatives (and leadership) can't be trusted.

What Real Retraining Looks Like

Real retraining isn't a two-hour workshop on "Working with AI." It's capability-building that maps directly to the system you're building:

- System mapping and workflow automation tools
- AI-enabled CRM and pipeline management
- Real-time data visualization and signal monitoring
- Low-code/no-code workflow platforms
- Working with automation systems and AI agents
- AI-human interaction design

When retraining is offered early, framed as a real career path, and backed by meaningful investment, people support it. When it's vague, delayed, or superficial, they quietly sabotage it.

AI-native businesses can't afford quiet resistance. They need operators who will push the system forward, own its success, and evolve with it.

That's why retraining isn't just a workforce strategy, it's system survival.

Operator's Log

> *"One of our portfolio companies leaned hard into AI to cut costs. They optimized back-office workflows and automated low-value processes. The P&L looked great, but they never invested in building differentiated, customer-facing capabilities. When the market shifted, they were left with a lean operation, with no defensible position. Efficiency without system advantage doesn't hold value at exit."*
>
> - Operating Partner, Multi-Sector PE Firm

Freeing up capacity is only part of the story. The harder question is whether that capacity actually turns into enterprise value. To capture real value, leadership must track where AI is changing the financial metrics, where does it affect revenue, margin, cash flow, and the pace of decision-making? This is where AI shifts from being operational to becoming a source of measurable, bankable value.

Chapter 34

AI VALUE CAPTURE

Turning AI Potential into EBITDA Reality

AI doesn't automatically create enterprise value. It creates potential.

Value Capture vs. Value Creation

AI discussions tend to focus on "value creation," the theoretical upside AI could deliver. Value capture is different; it's sharper, more demanding. It's locking in gains that show up in the financials, affect valuation, and stand up to buyer scrutiny.

If the value isn't captured, AI becomes just another slide in the deck instead of a line item in the financial model.

Capturing AI value comes down to four interconnected disciplines:

1. Process Change

AI can radically change how work gets done, but the system only holds if the organization adopts the change and locks it in.

Example: AI prioritizes inbound leads based on buyer intent, but if the sales team ignores the scoring and sticks to old habits, nothing changes.

Capture Requirements:

- Align KPIs and incentives with the new workflows.
- Train teams and provide ongoing change support.
- Deprecate legacy processes that compete with AI.
- Find and eliminate handoff points that slow the work.
- Focus on relieving bottlenecks and system constraints.
- Measure adoption rates and system usage consistently.

For private equity-backed businesses, this step has to move fast. If the process changes don't land quickly, AI gains erode before they show up in board reports.

2. Decision Enhancement

AI surfaces new insights and accelerates decision cycles, but intelligence without action doesn't drive value.

Example: AI identifies customer segments with higher lifetime value, but if marketing budgets and sales strategies don't adjust, the insight is wasted.

Capture Requirements:

- Integrate AI output into weekly operating reviews and monthly business rhythms.
- Clarify decision rights, who acts on which insights and when.
- Build feedback loops to track whether decisions actually improve outcomes.
- Train managers to interpret and act on AI recommendations.

For executives, decision acceleration needs to be quickly visible in board packs and operating discussions. That's what shifts AI from potential to realized financial impact.

3. Structural Reinforcement

Even when AI works, it can quietly unravel if the systems aren't built to sustain it.

Example: AI-generated marketing content may lead to revenue gains, but if it isn't embedded into the content management system with the right governance, the gains evaporate.

Capture Requirements:

- Integrate successful AI models directly into core business systems.
- Establish governance processes that guard model performance and output quality.
- Build proprietary data assets that keep the AI system improving.
- Document and systematize workflows so AI gains can scale and transfer across teams.

Private equity-backed businesses must build for scale. If the AI solution only works in one pocket of the business, it won't hold through diligence.

4. Cultural Enablement

Process, decisions, and structure will eventually collapse without cultural reinforcement. The business must evolve how it thinks, how it measures success, and how it leads.

Capture Requirements:

- Build AI fluency across leadership and frontline teams.
- Incentivize cross-functional outcomes, not local wins.
- Make AI progress part of the operating cadence, not a side project.
- Ensure governance cadences include cultural health checks, not just system audits.
- Encourage teams to challenge old metrics when AI opens up new ways to measure success.

Without cultural enablement, the system slowly drifts back to manual work, and AI fades into shelf ware.

Common Value Leakage Points

- **Initiative Fatigue:** Teams lose momentum when AI projects take too long or feel like extra work.
- **Organizational Resistance:** Middle management blocks adoption when AI threatens existing processes or power structures.
- **Technical Debt:** AI systems break when pilot-stage builds aren't ready for production-scale complexity.
- **Measurement Gaps:** Success metrics that aren't tied to business outcomes create false confidence in AI value.

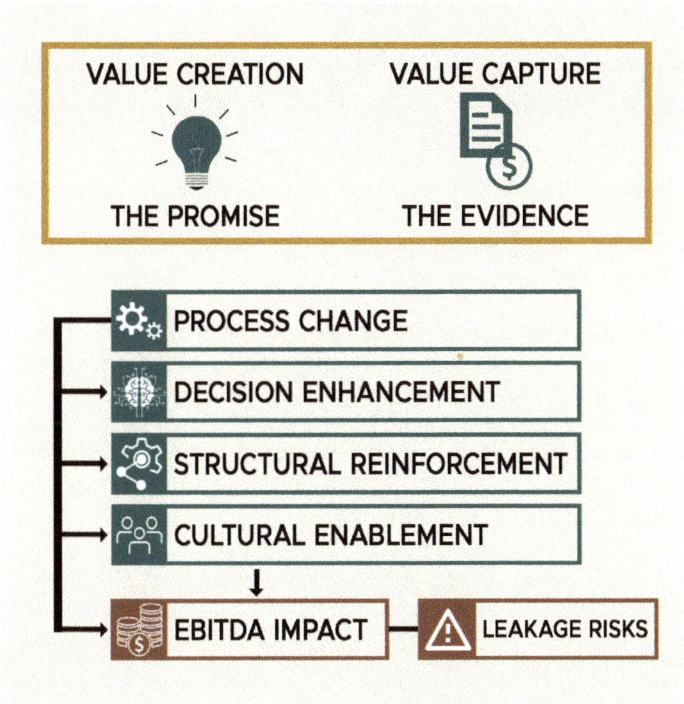

The PE-Specific Playbook

For private equity-backed companies, value capture isn't optional. It has to happen quickly, visibly, and in ways that stand up under diligence.

- **Tie AI to Financial Models:** Every AI initiative should connect to revenue, margin, or efficiency improvements that owners care about.
- **Embed AI in Operating Rhythms:** AI insights should show up in weekly reviews, monthly discussions, and quarterly cycles.
- **Document ROI Rigorously:** Track and report AI impact with the same scrutiny applied to other capital investments.
- **Design for Scale:** Build AI solutions that can grow across functions and geographies without starting over.

Case Example: AI-Driven Demand Forecasting

A portfolio company in industrials used AI to improve demand forecasting accuracy by 15%, reducing working capital tied up in excess inventory. But the real value came from capturing that improvement:

- AI forecasts were integrated directly into the ERP system.
- Finance teams adjusted inventory buffers based on AI recommendations.
- Procurement workflows were updated to use AI-driven lead time predictions.
- Supplier relationships were restructured around more accurate demand signals.

Result: An $11M reduction in working capital that was documented, measured, and repeatable. That improvement showed up in deal models as fact, not projection.

Deploying AI is a bet. Capturing the value is the payoff. However, it only holds if it's applied to the right levers. The next step is finding financial wins that actually move the needle.

Chapter 35

THE QUICK WIN MACHINE

Building, Prioritizing, and Protecting System Momentum

Wins accelerate progress, build confidence, and unlock early value. If the wrong wins are picked, or the right ones are rushed, the system quietly weakens while everyone is busy celebrating the things that don't really matter.

There are three outcomes the machine must deliver:

1. **Build the Core:** Plan and execute the development of the primary system, the intelligent core that powers the business.
2. **Deliver Secondary System Gains:** Capture fast, measurable improvements in secondary systems, support functions that drive operational efficiency and business stability.
3. **Enable Differentiation:** Build primary system capabilities that make customer-facing differentiation possible later.

Core First

The primary system is the intelligent business operating system. It's where scalable, adaptive capacity lives. This is where the system gains the ability to sense live signals, make decisions in motion, and adjust without manual intervention.

Don't make the mistake of chasing visible customer-facing features too early. The real early gains in the primary system aren't what the customer sees today. They are the core capabilities that will allow customer-specific differentiation tomorrow.

Plan the sequence of core capabilities development in an order that deliberately unlocks value opportunities in the secondary system. Building the core in the right sequence creates openings for rapid efficiency gains in finance, sales, procurement, reporting, and support, without starving the primary build.

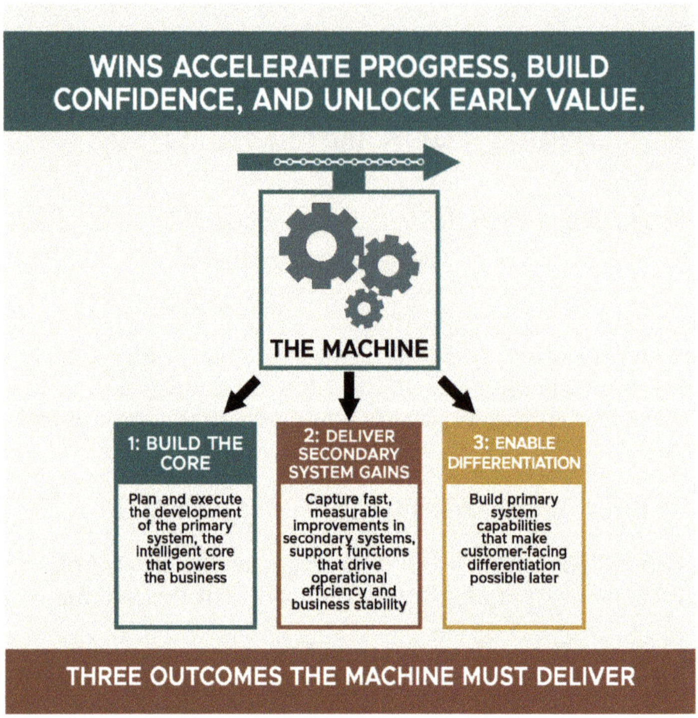

Deliver Secondary System Gains in Parallel

Improvements in the secondary system, the business support functions, and internal operations can and should run in parallel with the core development.

Secondary system gains often:

- Improve reporting speed and accuracy.
- Stabilize procurement, billing, and support functions.
- Deliver measurable efficiency gains that free up capacity.

For example:

A data integration layer built for customer workflows can also enable immediate improvements in financial reporting or internal support ticket automation.

When primary system progress directly unlocks meaningful gains in the secondary system, those primary builds should move up the priority list.

Secondary system projects that rely on primary system progress are the right targets. Cut cosmetic automations or low-value process tweaks that pull resources away from the core build.

Move Toward Differentiation

Customer-facing differentiation comes next, but only after the core is complete enough to support it.

The core makes scalable personalization, intelligent pricing, and adaptive customer support possible. Without it, early revenue moves collapse under scale.

When the core is ready, differentiation projects should:

- Strengthen pricing power
- Improve retention with intelligent, customer-specific experiences
- Broaden the addressable market
- Build system intelligence that compounds over time

These are the moves that hold up under diligence and drive valuation.

Guard the Sequence

The sequence is not a guideline; it's a structural discipline:

When leadership gets distracted, when pressure builds, or when the focus shifts to chasing numbers, the sequence holds the system together.

Managing Investor Pressure

PE owners will always press for faster results. That pressure can quietly collapse the primary system without disciplined leadership.

To hold the sequence:

Keep the primary system build visible. It should lead board packs and operating reviews.

Track resource allocation between core build and secondary improvements in plain sight.

Show early progress, but always in the right lane, secondary system gains that don't compromise the core.

Show them how the road to the future can bring benefits today. Use developing intelligence capabilities on initiatives that are directly tied to the current strategy, i.e., sales and marketing, customer support, and technical debt reduction.

Show them the future with data. Project when internal improvements will land and when system capacity will unlock but stay grounded. This is not the time to sell vision, it's the time to sell reality.

Build What Holds

Showing early results keeps the system moving, but not all progress carries the same weight. Focus on the work that delivers measurable financial impact and improvements that can be tracked, reported, and directly tied to key financial metrics.

Showing results in the right sequence keeps the plan on track without compromising its long-term strength. Let's look at examples of how to apply some AI capabilities before the core is fully built, before the system reaches maturity. The next step is finding the fastest path to early victory, where tomorrow's AI can start solving today's problems right now.

DOWNLOAD: AI Quick Win Scorecard
The AI Quick Win Scorecard provides a systematic method for evaluating and prioritizing AI opportunities that can deliver measurable business value quickly . This framework prevents organizations from pursuing "interesting" AI projects that don't align with strategic priorities or create genuine business impact.
www.theaifix.online

Chapter 36

WALMART, A QUICK WIN USE CASE

Quick Wins While Building the Core AI Intelligence

For private equity–backed companies navigating the hard growth path, the challenge is balancing the need for immediate, visible results with the discipline to build durable, defensible systems. Walmart offers a standout example. The retail giant secured operational quick wins that boosted performance in the short term while simultaneously building a scalable AI platform to compound value over the long haul. This sequencing allowed Walmart to pivot from tactical efficiency gains to strategic differentiation, exactly the trajectory PE operators should aim for.

1. Quick Win: Holiday Inventory Optimization (2019–2023)

Walmart implemented an AI-powered inventory management system capable of analyzing historical sales, local weather, macroeconomic trends, and real-time search activity to forecast demand. By placing holiday stock in optimal locations across stores and distribution centers, Walmart improved on-shelf availability, reduced markdowns, and protected margins during the peak season (Walmart Global Tech, 2023).

2. Core Build: 'Element' Machine Learning Platform (2022–2025)

While delivering those operational gains, Walmart invested in Element, a proprietary, multi-cloud–agnostic machine learning platform. Element provides enterprise-grade tooling for data ingestion, model development, automated deployment, resource provisioning, cost attribution, and governance. It serves as the AI backbone for scaling use cases across functions, avoiding the fragmentation of one-off solutions (Walmart Global Tech, 2022).

3. From Operational Wins to Differentiation

With Element in place, Walmart expanded into higher-order AI capabilities: generative-AI search, real-time forecasting, intelligent last-mile delivery, and AI-driven merchandising insights. This evolution shifted AI from a supporting efficiency role to a driver of customer-facing differentiation (Walmart Global Tech, 2024).

How to Copy This in Your PE Portfolio

Ship a visible, measurable win fast - Identify a high-impact operational pain point, inventory, lead prioritization, or quality control, and solve it with a minimal AI pilot.

Build the intelligent infrastructure underneath – Stand up a scalable, governed AI platform, standardizing data flows, deployment, and monitoring across the business.

Use the platform to layer differentiation – Leverage your core to deliver harder-to-copy, customer-facing capabilities that directly influence valuation.

References

Walmart Global Tech (2023) Walmart's AI-Powered Inventory System Brightens the Holidays.

https://tech.walmart.com/content/walmart-global-tech/en_us/blog/post/walmarts-ai-powered-inventory-system-brightens-the-holidays.html

Walmart Global Tech (2022) Element: Walmart's Machine Learning Platform.

https://medium.com/walmartglobaltech/element-walmarts-machine-learning-platform-b8a1f7870784

Walmart Global Tech (2024) Walmart's Element: A Machine Learning Platform Like No Other.

https://tech.walmart.com/content/walmart-global-tech/en_us/blog/post/walmarts-element-a-machine-learning-platform-like-no-other.html

Chapter 37

THE FASTEST PATH TO EARLY RESULTS

Winning Now with the Tools of the Future

AI system builds don't happen in a vacuum. While the primary system progresses, the rest of the business keeps moving. Operations don't stop. Customers don't wait. Boards don't press pause.

The fastest way to show early results is to apply new AI capabilities the moment they become available, not just for the future system, but for the business as it runs today. Using tomorrow's AI to improve today's operations shows owners and investors that the system is already creating a measurable impact across key financial metrics.

The Role of Different AI Types

Different AI support different layers of this architecture. Intelligent systems rarely rely on just one approach. They combine AI types to create a flexible, scalable capability stack.

Traditional AI (Predictive Models and Rule-Based Systems)

Traditional AI often looks like the natural starting point because it's been around longer and feels more mature. In practice, it's a heavier lift. Predictive models need structured data, integration into core systems, and teams capable of maintaining them.

- **Strengths:** Supports automated decision flows, dynamic prioritization, and continuous learning. Manages predictable, structured decisions like churn prediction, demand forecasting, and pricing optimization.
- **Limitations:** Operates well in stable environments but struggles when conditions shift dramatically.

Where Traditional AI Fits

Traditional AI is the quiet workhorse of intelligent systems. It delivers reliable value when conditions are structured and data is consistent. In practice, this means:

- Early Deployment: While data is being cleaned and structured, predictive models can be applied to areas where history is a strong guide, such as demand forecasting, fraud detection, or inventory optimization.
- Parallel Value Creation: Traditional AI runs best in the background alongside generative AI pilots, providing a stream of reliable, incremental gains while GenAI experiments capture more visible wins.
- Foundation for Autonomy: Agentic AI depends on high-quality signals to act responsibly. Traditional AI models often provide those signals, forecasts, scores, and risk flags, that agentic systems use as inputs.

Think of traditional AI as the stabilizer: it creates confidence and measurable progress before the more experimental or adaptive layers are ready to scale.

Generative AI (Language Models and Content Generators)

Generative AI often leapfrogs traditional AI as the practical entry point. It can be bolted into existing workflows with little technical setup.

- **Strengths:** Synthesizes activity into natural language, generates content, and expands human-system interaction. Works immediately in areas like marketing, sales support, customer proposals, or service chat where the "time-to-value" is measured in days or weeks.
- **Limitations:** Highly visible, but not reliable for making business-critical decisions. Needs to be paired with governance to avoid errors scaling out of control.

Agentic AI (Goal-Seeking, Autonomous Agents)

Agentic AI extends the stack into autonomy, automating workflows end to end.

- **Strengths:** Pursues objectives across multiple steps, adapts in real time, and closes gaps between functions.
- **Limitations:** Requires strong guardrails and trusted signals (often from traditional AI) to prevent drift or unintended outcomes.

SYSTEM CAPABILITY	TRADITIONAL AI	GENERATIVE AI	AGENTIC AI
Real-Time Data Capture	X	✓	✓
Integrated Data Sources	✓	✓	✓
Automated Decision Flows	✓	Limited	✓
Context-Aware Processing	✓	Limited	✓
Continuous Learning Loops	Some	Limited	✓
Dynamic Prioritization Engines	Some	X	✓
Cross-Functional Visibility	Limited	✓	✓

Capability Mapping

An intelligent system is rarely built on a single type of AI. The strongest systems layer:

- Generative AI for quick entry and visible productivity gains,
- Traditional AI for structured, predictive strength once data foundations mature,
- Agentic AI for real-time adaptability and autonomy when guardrails exist.

How to Sequence Deployment

The sequencing reflects reality, not just theory:

1. Quick Wins with Generative AI. Deploy GenAI where infrastructure isn't a blocker, marketing, customer service, and sales support. Early results are visible and buy leadership confidence.
2. Structured Gains with Traditional AI. Once data pipelines improve, bring in predictive models for forecasting, pricing, and

risk. These stabilize operations and expand credibility.

3. Autonomy with Agentic AI. With signals and governance in place, agents automate cross-functional workflows at scale.

Apply the Future to Today's Business

The message to owners and investors is clear: the system isn't just preparing for future advantage, it's improving today's operations in real time, with visible financial impact.

Early AI deployment shows:

- Immediate productivity from GenAI pilots,
- Structured operational efficiency from traditional AI,
- Workflow acceleration and adaptability from agentic AI,
- A practical preview of what the fully built system will deliver.

This is how you buy time, earn confidence, and keep leadership engaged while the primary system matures.

A Word of Caution

Focusing on the wrong problems wastes effort and weakens credibility. Aim improvements at the pressure points that actually constrain the business. If customer churn is already low, customer support may not need immediate AI attention. If sales is overloaded with leads, generating more isn't the priority—improving conversion and capacity is.

AI can shape tomorrow's business, but the smartest early wins come from applying the right type of AI at the right moment to the problems that matter today. Results that don't land in the financials won't hold leadership attention or buyer confidence. Tightening that connection is the first step in value capture.

Chapter 38

FINDING FINANCIAL WINS THAT MATTER

Where AI Works: Targeting the Four Value Pillars

AI only generates returns when pointed at the right parts of the business.

The fastest way to create momentum? Embed AI where the business spends, earns, and leaks the most value. Put AI to work in places where it makes a measurable difference.

Early financial returns can look like the perfect answer. They are measurable. They are visible. They show up in savings reports that make owners happy. In this context, financial wins are process improvements and systems optimization that impact financial metrics (the ones that matter).

The right financial AI initiatives can stabilize cash flow, improve margins, and free up working capital without pulling the business off track. They create breathing room, and the organization keeps moving towards the prize. They keep the energy up. They keep the business in motion. They give operating teams something to show while the more important work is still under construction.

Consider Inputs, not Outputs

Before we rush into applying AI across the business, it's critical to shift perspective.

This isn't a financial review. We're not analyzing the income statement. We're examining how value flows through the business, how activities and decisions translate into sales, cash, revenue, gross margin, and net income.

Financial metrics are outputs. This chapter is about the inputs.

Cost Is the Common Denominator

The goal isn't to chase novelty or fall in love with automation for its own sake. It's to find the specific functions and processes where AI can create *real*, measurable improvement.

Here's the core idea:

Every part of a business creates costs or suffers from constraints. Sometimes both. Cost comes in two forms: money and time. The third factor, constraints, can add to either.

AI creates value when it reduces time or cost or relieves the constraints.

To do that, examine value flow through these three lenses:

1. **Cost** – Where can AI automate or streamline high-cost processes? This is where initial traction is found, for example, in back-office functions like G&A or service-heavy COGS.
2. **Time** – Where is the flow of value delayed because of inefficient processes, rework, or human bandwidth?
3. **Constraint** – Where are teams, systems, or execution bottlenecked? These are the leverage points, places where improving throughput unlocks outsized impact.

Using this lens, let's walk through the operational drivers behind core financial metrics, cash, COGS, G&A, and sales.

Finding Where AI Delivers the Highest ROI

Examining the Real Value Pillars

Where do we point AI? Not every business function offers the same return. Some processes are already efficient. Others are too small to matter. And some are high-stakes bottlenecks where even modest improvements compound dramatically.

The aim here is to build a prioritized, high-impact roadmap. We see how to assess each function for AI readiness, how to frame ROI in operational terms, and how to link AI use cases to the value creation thesis.

Now, let's begin where runway matters most: cash.

Cash Management:

The Silent Choke Point

In cash management, speed beats savings. Accelerating when you invoice, when you collect, and how fast cash moves through the system has more impact than squeezing costs alone. Businesses that tighten accounts receivable while managing accounts payable delays put cash to work faster, and that's where the real advantage sits.

This is where AI delivers muted but powerful leverage, not with polished dashboards, but with early warnings, smarter forecasts, and sharper working capital decisions.

Why Cash Management Needs AI?

It's easy to find finance teams that still live in Excel. Forecasting models are fragile. Collections are reactive. The real-time cash position doesn't connect to payables. People make short-term decisions based on lagging reports.

AI doesn't need to replace the finance function. It just needs to make it faster, more precise, and more predictive.

Applied correctly, AI can:

- Improve cash flow visibility and forecast accuracy
- Detect risk in customer payments or supplier terms
- Optimize collections sequencing and payment scheduling
- Show hidden working capital inefficiencies
- Provide early warnings for liquidity pressure

Cash is the constraint that compounds when ignored, and the advantage that compounds when controlled.

The Real Impact

AI in cash management delivers foresight. It provides a live, system-wide view of where cash is moving, where it's likely to stall, and where policy decisions could unlock millions in trapped capital. Done right, this shifts the finance function from a record-keeping team to an operational nerve center, one that knows when to push, when to slow, and when to shift gears.

But cash management doesn't stop at flow and timing. AI can also optimize how cash is put to work. Intelligent systems can monitor exchange rates, interest rates, and money markets in real time, recommending when to move cash, where to hold it, and how to maximize returns. AI can weigh options across short-term investments, debt reduction, working capital priorities, and even owner distributions, providing leadership with clear, timely trade-offs.

Margin buys valuation, but cash buys time.

General & Administrative (G&A):

The Cost of Coordination—Where AI Needs a Measured Approach

Typically, sales and G&A are combined on an income statement, SG&A. We have deliberately separated sales, and the reason will be plain later.

G&A often flies under the radar until it starts quietly chewing through 15–25% of revenue. It's packed with essential, repeatable, rules-based processes, the kind that look ripe for automation. And while that's true many times, a critical nuance often gets missed: improving efficiency doesn't automatically reduce cost.

Counterintuitively, cost reduction is not the benefit of applying AI to G&A. It is speeding up the flow of value.

G&A labor is indirect. If AI speeds up a process, say, reconciling expenses, reviewing contracts, or drafting documents, true savings are only seen if the number of people doing that work is reduced or their time is reallocated to higher-impact initiatives that are connected to sales and COGS. Otherwise, it's just creating surplus capacity.

Therefore, applying AI to G&A requires deliberate intent. Ask: *What are we achieving?* If it's cost reduction, is there a plan to redeploy or eliminate redundant effort? If it's speed, will that speed free up downstream constraints in revenue, COGS, or customer experience?

There are G&A functions where speed and precision create real enterprise value. For instance:

- Errors in billing and invoicing delay collections and choke cash flow
- Delays in legal contract review can slow deals and stall revenue
- A faster HR function speeds hiring into revenue-generating roles
- Inefficient vendor contracts inflate COGS and G&A unnecessarily

- Poor forecasting leads to mis-allocated capital and shortfalls

These are not hypothetical gains. They're real, measurable improvements, *if* the goals are clear from the outset.

The chapter "**The Efficiency Paradox**" explores what happens when surplus capacity is created without a strategy for how to use it. Here, we simply flag the importance of thinking one step ahead: improving a task isn't enough unless what that improvement is supposed to unlock is known.

The Real Impact

When deployed with strategic clarity, AI in G&A is cost containment, but it removes the drag that slows everything else down. That means faster decisions, fewer bottlenecks, or more bandwidth for initiatives that *drive* revenue or margin. But none of that happens automatically.

AI in G&A works best when it's aligned not just to process efficiency, but to business impact. The aim isn't doing more with less. It's on doing the right things faster, clearing the way for the rest of the company to move.

Gross Margins/COGS

The Front Line of Margin—Where AI Earns Its Keep

Now, COGS. This is where we lose value the fastest and recover it the fastest. Another name for COGS is the cost of execution. Here we want to speed up execution and reduce the cost of doing so.

In a software business, COGS isn't an abstraction, it's the core machinery. There, employees design, build, test, deliver, document, and often implement or support products. Every inefficiency in this system is a margin leak. Every delay, handoff, or avoidable error quietly compounds into increased cost of delivery. The good news? These are exactly the kinds of structured, repeatable processes that AI excels at optimizing.

Why COGS Now?

COGS is where AI drives the most immediate and measurable impact, without requiring a total business model rewrite. Applied correctly, AI can:

- Increase engineering velocity without increasing engineering headcount
- Improve software quality and reduce post-release defects

- Prioritize roadmaps and test suites based on data, not instinct
- Shorten development cycles and reduce delivery risk
- Reduce technical debt with code optimization and refactoring
- Automate documentation and reduce technical overhead
- Optimize implementation timelines and lower onboarding costs

This isn't hype, it's unit economics.

AI applied to COGS isn't just "transformative." It's practical, fast, and defensible. These are systems that already generate data, operate at scale, and rely heavily on repeatable patterns. That makes them ideal candidates for AI-powered augmentation or automation.

Sales

Turning Potential into Pipeline—Sharpening the Commercial Engine with AI

Sales initiate the value creation process. It generates the first signals of customer demand and sets the conditions for revenue, cash flow, and long-term engagement. The sales process functions best when it operates with structure, discipline, and visibility. Performance is measured by consistency in execution and clarity in forecasting.

AI supports sales operations by reducing noise, highlighting patterns, and reinforcing high-impact behaviors. Its value lies in strengthening the sales process through better prioritization and timely insights.

Sales as a System

The sales process begins upstream, well before contracts are signed. Activities such as market outreach, lead qualification, and engagement tracking form the foundation of the pipeline. Low-quality leads, overloaded pipelines, and limited understanding of what drives conversion slow many sales environments.

AI introduces structure to this early activity. By analyzing historical outcomes and real-time behavior, it helps sales organizations identify where to focus, when to engage, and which opportunities show the greatest likelihood of success. Sales become a cycle of input, insight, and adjustment.

Sales performance influences not only current-period revenue but also longer-term value drivers: retention, efficiency, and scalability. The financial implications extend beyond bookings and affect how reliably growth turns into equity value.

Operational Outcomes

AI guides sellers toward prospects with real potential, clarifies pipeline health, and reduces time spent on low-probability opportunities. These changes support measurable improvements in sales operations:

- Sales professionals focus activity on qualified leads
- Managers base coaching on observed performance patterns
- Revenue forecasts reflect data-driven assumptions

Sales, when consistently executed and supported by actionable insight, become the foundation for sustainable business performance. AI contributes to this foundation by accelerating decisions, strengthening discipline, and linking commercial activity to enterprise outcomes.

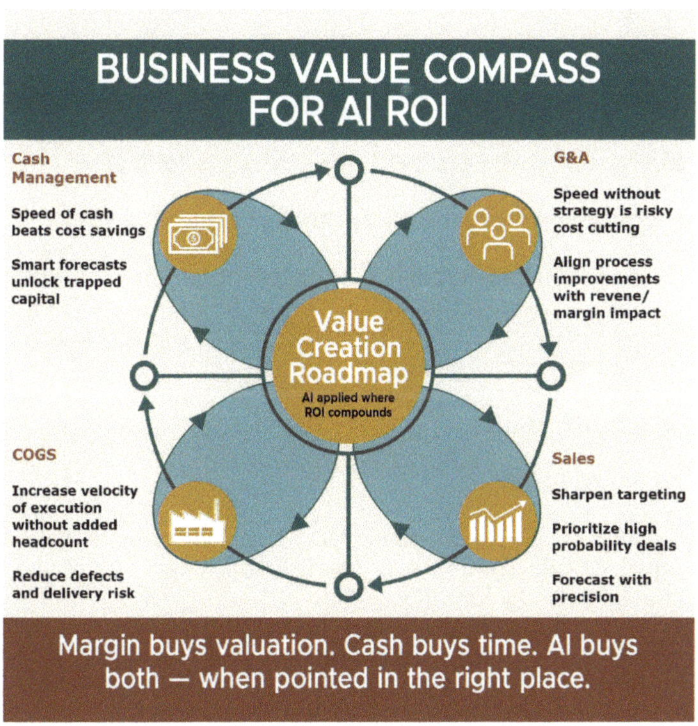

What About Revenue?

Revenue is one of the most closely watched financial metrics. It drives valuation, signals growth, and anchors strategy. But it's often misunderstood.

Revenue is an *output*, not a function. And when applying AI, it's critical to understand what that means.

Revenue Is Not Sales

Claims like "AI helped us grow revenue" will trace back to lead targeting, improved conversion rates, or expanded marketing reach, not direct changes to revenue recognition. Revenue is an accounting milestone, a number recorded after the sale, based on how much of the contract or service has been delivered.

Revenue Is a Measurement of Execution

In every business model, revenue is recognized differently:

- **SaaS** - Evenly across the subscription period.
- **Time & Materials** - Based on hours billed and work delivered.
- **Fixed-fee software projects** - As a percentage of completion.
- **License delivery** - When software is handed over.
- **Professional services** - On milestone or stage completion.

Revenue recognition is a compliance activity. Increasing revenue recognition in any period means to:

1. **Sell more** and/or,
2. **Execute faster.**

AI cannot rewrite revenue recognition rules. But it *can* help to reach the recognition milestone faster. Put differently:

Revenue is not recognized when a contract is signed. It's recognized when a product or service is delivered. And delivery lives in COGS.

So, don't ask, "Where do I apply AI to improve revenue?" Ask, "How can I improve my sales engine and execution system?"

The real AI opportunity lies in shortening the time between *promise made* (sales) and *promise kept* (delivery).

Understanding where to find value is the first step. Knowing where to look is critical, but it's not enough. The real challenge is knowing what to look for, what signals matter, what cost drivers are actually controllable, and where AI can move the needle. The next step is breaking down the cost structures and identifying the levers that can unlock meaningful gains.

Chapter 39

WE KNOW WHERE TO LOOK, BUT WHAT ARE WE LOOKING FOR?

Translating Financial Signals into Operational Targets for AI

In the previous chapters, we identified where to look, COGS, G&A, sales, and cash management. Recognizing the right category isn't enough. It's time to drill down into the layers beneath those categories to find where cost is hiding, where time is leaking, where constraints live, and where AI might offer meaningful improvement.

Begin with the Value Metric, Not the Org Chart

Don't start by asking where to apply AI to "Sales" or "Customer Support." Instead, start with the value metric. If the strategic priority is cash flow, ask: *What are the desired outputs and what are the processes that affect how cash enters or leaves the business?*

If the priority is gross margin, ask: *Where are the costs incurred? Where are the avoidable delays? What processes are most time-consuming and labor-intensive?*

Start by treating each financial lever like a flag. If G&A is high as a percentage of revenue, that's a signal. If COGS has ballooned but delivery timelines haven't shortened, that's another. But don't look for AI use cases yet. Look for material operational pressure points. AI doesn't fix vague. It optimizes the specific.

Step 1: Quantify the Lever

Pick a lever, say, COGS. Ask two simple questions:

- What is the total dollar amount of COGS over the last 12 months?
- What percentage of revenue does that represent?

Then compare this against industry benchmarks. Is it in line, slightly bloated, or way off? No AI yet. Just judgment and financial context.

Step 2: Decide If There's Room to Move

Is there belief (and data to support it) inside the organization that these costs can be improved without harming quality, delivery, or customer satisfaction? If not, stop here. Don't deploy AI to fine-tune a system that isn't asking for improvement.

If yes, move on.

Step 3: Break the Cost into Components

Take that high-level line item, COGS, for example, and segment it:

- Labor
- Third-party licenses
- Specialized equipment
- Cloud infrastructure

Now ask again: where is the money hiding? What seems bloated, or fragile, or ripe for scrutiny?

Step 4: Link to Functions and Processes

Once a suspect cost category is identified, trace it back to the operational functions and then to the specific processes driving it. For example:

Example: COGS is 40% of revenue, and 70% of that is labor. Digging deeper, it's now clear that the software engineering team spends 25% of its time waiting for test environment availability and test data. The bottleneck isn't their skills; it's the delay between code completion and test execution.

This moves the focus from a broad concept like "developer efficiency" to a specific execution bottleneck: test environment provisioning and data management. AI can mitigate this constraint by predicting test cycles, auto-provisioning environments, or generating synthetic test data, targeted solutions tied to real throughput.

Where Systems Thinking Fits

This example evaluates cost independently, but we have previously discussed the bigger picture, systems thinking. Improving one area in isolation will do nothing if it's upstream from a bottleneck or downstream from a constraint. During the prioritization activity, consider not just the dollar amounts, but how processes interact. A flashy initiative that promises to reduce costs in one silo may fall flat if another part of the business can't keep up.

Before getting eager about applying AI to speed up one function, trace its upstream inputs and downstream outputs. Will faster execution in one area overwhelm a slower function next in line? Will automating a task remove vital manual checks that others depend on? Fixing a single step is meaningless if the rest of the process breaks under pressure. Successful operators think in flows, not fragments. AI should follow that same logic. This is the most important concept in any business, Systems Thinking.

Even if, after uncovering areas where cost savings or efficiency gains seem possible, this is not the time to choose to apply AI. A problem may have been found, but AI might not be the right tool to solve it. Some issues are better addressed through process redesign, better training, system upgrades, or simply stronger management discipline. Applying AI to a broken or misaligned process can automate dysfunction, not eliminate it. The point of these steps is to surface operational friction and financial drag, not to prescribe solutions. That comes next. First, confirm there's something worth fixing. Then determine whether AI is the right mechanism to fix it.

Is AI the Right Solution?

Finding operational friction is a part of the work. The next step is to decide if the problem you've uncovered is a good fit for AI.

Before moving forward, run a sharp test: Does this problem actually need AI?

Here's what to look for:

- **Complex, Variable, or Data-Heavy Workflows:** Problems with high variability, large data sets, or complex decision paths are where AI adds the most value. Static, rule-based tasks can usually be solved with simpler automation or process fixes.
- **Bottlenecks Driven by Decision Speed or Information Overload:** If the problem is slow human decision-making or struggling to process too much data, AI can help accelerate decisions and surface insights.
- **Patterns That Humans Can't See Fast Enough:** AI excels at finding hidden signals in large volumes of data, especially where those patterns would take too long or be too subtle for humans to track.

- **Repetitive Tasks with Complex Inputs:** Standard repetitive work can often be automated with basic tools. But if the task is repetitive and relies on messy, dynamic, or multi-source data, AI becomes more useful.
- **Work That Benefits from Continuous Learning:** Processes that improve over time with more exposure to new data (like predictive maintenance, demand forecasting, or intelligent routing) are well-suited for AI-driven improvement.

If a problem doesn't meet these conditions, applying AI might overcomplicate the solution, drive up cost, or simply automate dysfunction.

The Quick Test:

Ask:

- *Is the core challenge speed, scale, complexity, or pattern recognition?*
- *Is this something that actually benefits from intelligent learning over time?*

If the answer is no, fix it without AI.

If the answer is yes, this is where AI can make a meaningful, measurable difference.

Systems thinking forces us to look beyond isolated fixes and trace how changes ripple through the business. But tracing the flow isn't enough. We need to understand which parts of the system actually move the numbers that matter to owners and boards. Not every improvement will show up in the financial model. The next step is to focus on the business levers that shift the SaaS metrics investors care about, and to ensure AI efforts are tied directly to those levers.

DOWNLOAD: AI Value Lever Analysis Tool
The tool provides a systematic approach to identify, evaluate, and prioritize AI opportunities across the four primary value levers: Sales, COGS, G&A, and Cash Management. Rather than pursuing AI initiatives randomly, this framework ensures strategic alignment with business objectives and maximum value creation potential.
www.theaifix.online

Chapter 40

LINKING CORE SAAS METRICS TO VALUE CREATION OBJECTIVES

How Core Business Levers Drive the Metrics That Matter

SaaS metrics like customer acquisition cost (CAC), CAC Payback, lifetime value (LTV), net revenue retention (NRR), and gross revenue retention (GRR) dominate dashboards and board packs. These are the metrics owners watch to judge progress, but these metrics don't move on their own. They move when the core business levers shift.

When AI initiatives directly influence these levers, they stop being back-office experiments; they become measurable proof points that investors trust.

Chasing better SaaS metrics without improving the value levers is wasted effort. Metrics are outcomes, not problems to solve in isolation.

The Fastest Path to Real Improvement:

- **To Lower CAC?** Tackle sales efficiency and SG&A waste.
- **To Improve LTV?** Focus on pricing, retention, and delivery margins.
- **To Accelerate CAC Payback?** Tighten cash collection and improve gross margin.
- **To Lift NRR and GRR?** Strengthen expansion and reduce churn with customer fit and delivery precision.

When selecting and prioritizing AI initiatives, consider their direct influence on these levers. If a project doesn't move a lever, it's not a priority.

Tune the System, Not the Dashboard

Trying to improve CAC without fixing sales execution is like polishing the dashboard while the engine misfires. Metrics follow when the system is tuned correctly, when cash discipline sharpens, sales execution tightens, gross margins improve, and delivery stabilizes.

Don't chase the number, fix the system that moves it. When the fundamentals are held, the metrics will follow, and so will enterprise value.

Connecting AI initiatives to the right SaaS metrics makes the work visible in the numbers that matter. But visibility is only part of the job. Leadership, owners, and buyers need to see those metrics show up in the rhythm of the business. The next step is building AI business reporting that keeps the right metrics in front of the right people, at the right time.

Chapter 41

AI BUSINESS REPORTING

From Snapshots to Live Intelligence

"Gary, do you have this month's board report package yet?"

I lost countless hours preparing the CEO's monthly board report, dozens of pages tailored to each board member's shifting demands, only to witness the package go largely unread. The payoff? An overly long meeting spent answering questions already buried in those untouched pages, and the uncomfortable moment when a question came up that no one saw coming.

Traditional business reporting is like trying to drive using the rearview mirror. Monthly dashboards, quarterly reviews, and annual planning cycles made sense when change moved slowly. ERP and BI systems have been the gold standard in this world, excellent at compiling clean, reconciled data, building dashboards, and generating reports that show what happened. They are lagging-indicator machines: invaluable for documenting performance, but too slow to warn you about what's unfolding right now.

AI-native businesses operate differently. Instead of waiting for a scheduled report, AI-powered reporting surfaces what's happening and what's likely to happen next, in real time. The emphasis shifts toward **leading indicators**, reducing the gap between a change in conditions and a management response.

Think of it this way:

- **ERP/BI** - "Here's what happened."
- **AI** - "Here's what's happening, and here's what will likely happen if you don't act."

That's the difference between a rearview mirror and an onboard navigation system. One shows where you've been; the other gives you a live readout of the road ahead and warns you before you miss the turn.

The Evolution from Static to Adaptive

Most companies still operate on legacy reporting cycles:

- Finance closes the books monthly and reports what happened
- Sales forecasts quarterly and hopes the pipeline holds
- Operations reviews performance after problems become visible
- Strategy gets reviewed annually, whether the market cooperates or not

AI-enhanced businesses replace that lag with a continuous feed of actionable intelligence. ERP and BI remain essential for record-keeping and compliance, but when AI is layered on top, the entire model becomes adaptive and forward-looking.

What Live Intelligence Looks Like

- **Customer Health Monitoring:** AI scans support tickets, usage patterns, and engagement signals to flag accounts at risk before renewal conversations even start. No more discovering dissatisfaction in a quarterly review.
- **Pipeline Intelligence:** Real-time analysis of deal velocity, stakeholder engagement, and competitive moves gives sales teams early warnings. Forecasting shifts from hope to probability.
- **Operational Flow Detection:** AI monitors delivery timelines, resource utilization, and workflow bottlenecks, identifying capacity constraints before they reach the customer. Prevention replaces reaction.
- **Market Signal Processing:** Automated tracking of competitive actions, customer sentiment, and industry shifts keeps leadership anchored in market reality instead of quarterly assumptions.

Why This Matters

Live intelligence delivers three critical advantages:

1. **Faster Response Time:** Problems surfaced in real time can be addressed before they hit the P&L. Customer churn gets prevented instead of explained. Market shifts get anticipated

instead of absorbed.

2. **Better Board Conversations:** Meetings focus on current conditions and how the business is adapting, not just on post-mortems of last quarter's performance.

3. **Less Guessing:** NLP interfaces let board members and executives ask their own questions on demand, getting up-to-the-minute answers without waiting for the next formal report.

Closing the Latency Gap

In any reporting system, there are two delays:

- **Data latency** — the time between an event and when it appears in a report.
- **Decision latency** — the time between seeing the data and acting on it.

ERP and BI shorten data latency to the limits of their reporting cycle, but decision latency still depends on how quickly leadership can access and interpret the data. AI compresses both. It streams operational signals in real time and can trigger alerts or recommendations the moment conditions change, giving leaders a chance to act before the window closes.

Bridging the Trust Gap

Boards and executives will only act on AI-driven insights if they trust them. That requires:

- **Data provenance:** Confidence in the source and accuracy of the data.
- **Explainability:** The ability to see why the AI flagged a trend or risk.
- **Feedback loops:** Continuous improvement as decisions and outcomes feed back into the model.

ERP and BI have earned trust through decades of reconciled, auditable data. AI reporting needs the same governance discipline if it's going to move from "interesting" to "actionable" in the boardroom.

The real breakthrough in AI-powered reporting isn't in compressing data latency, it's in what happens next. Closing the gap between knowing and doing is where most boards stumble. You can have the sharpest predictive tool in the market, but if the people making decisions still use instinct and habit, they will miss the turn every time. Which brings us to the harder problem: not the tools, but the behavior that governs how they're used.

The Reporting Evolution

The strongest reporting frameworks combine AI-powered signal detection with leadership's ability to interpret context and act. When that combination is in place, reporting shifts from documenting the past to navigating the future. Progress becomes visible in real time, and when the board asks, "How soon will this matter?" you can point to the indicators that show the impact as it unfolds.

DOWNLOAD: AI ROI Reporting Workbook
Effective measurement systems are critical for demonstrating AI value, optimizing performance, and guiding strategic decisions. This framework provides comprehensive approaches to measuring AI success across technical, business, and organizational dimensions while enabling continuous improvement through data-driven iteration.
www.theaifix.online

Chapter 42

THE BOARDROOM

From Insight to Action

Installing AI-driven reporting is the easy part. Getting a board to change how it thinks, asks questions, and makes decisions in real time, that's the knife fight. The behavior gap isn't about understanding the data; it's about breaking decades of muscle memory built on quarterly cycles, siloed updates, and risk-averse pacing. Without a shift in boardroom habits, AI becomes an expensive mirror, reflecting back all the same blind spots you had before, only in higher definition.

The promise of AI-powered reporting isn't the dashboard. It's the decision that happens in time to make a difference.

That's where the wheels often come off. Not because the AI missed something, but because the board did.

Why the Data Isn't Enough

Boards like to think they make data-driven decisions. In reality, most make data-supported decisions, the conclusion comes first, the evidence gets pulled in later. AI doesn't magically fix that. If anything, real-time signals make the behavior gap more visible:

- A cross-functional risk appears in the live feed.
- The discussion still goes round the table function-by-function.
- By the time the dots are joined, the window to act has closed.

The obstacle isn't the technology. It's the habits.

The Real Latency Problem

In the reporting chapter, we looked at data latency and decision latency. AI can crush both, but only if boards change the way they engage:

- From presentation to interrogation: Instead of passively receiving a board pack, directors need to probe, challenge, and cross-connect insights in real time.

- From functional silos to integrated thinking: When an AI risk alert hits finance, it should be finance and sales and operations weighing in, not three separate updates an hour apart.
- From "we'll discuss it next time" to "we'll decide it now": Live intelligence loses value every day it sits in an action list.

The Chair's Role in Behavior Change

ERP and BI adoption was about getting clean data into the room. AI adoption is about getting the right conversations into the room. That is a Chair's job.

A Chair who wants AI to matter will:

1. Set the expectation — real-time insights are not "for information"; they are for immediate consideration.
2. Change the meeting cadence — no more quarterly strategy bolt-ons; instead, use shorter, more frequent AI-informed decision sessions.
3. Enforce cross-functional accountability — when AI shows a risk in one area, the discussion must include every function that will feel the impact.

Without this leadership from the Chair, AI becomes just another dashboard: admired, ignored, and eventually left to gather digital dust.

Boardroom Behavior Plays That Work

Here are a few practical shifts that close the behavior gap:

- Pre-meeting AI synthesis: Have the system generate a single-page cross-functional brief 24 hours before the meeting. Require every director to come prepared with one question it raised for them.
- Hot-seat scenarios: When a risk or opportunity is flagged, the Chair randomly picks a director to outline an immediate response, then opens the floor. It keeps everyone engaged — and honest about whether they've absorbed the data.
- AI-informed "What if?" drills: Dedicate part of the agenda to running one scenario forward using live data. Example: "If this supplier fails in 90 days, what's our revenue impact, and what

do we do today to mitigate it?"

- Live decision logging: Record which AI-driven signals were acted on, which were ignored, and why. Review the log quarterly, it's hard to dodge accountability when the record shows a pattern of missed opportunities.

Making It Stick

Behavioral change at board level doesn't happen by accident. It needs:

- Incentives — show how faster, better-timed decisions protect or grow value.
- Transparency — directors should see the results of their decisions (or indecision) in the same live feed that surfaced the issue.
- Cultural permission — directors must feel safe questioning assumptions in real time, even if it derails the planned agenda.

The AI can provide the signals.

The Chair can demand the change.

The board has to choose whether to take the turn in the road, or miss it entirely.

Chapter 43

HOW LONG DO WE HAVE TO WAIT?

Setting Realistic Timelines for AI Value Capture

One of the first questions that shows up in private equity-backed businesses when AI enters the conversation is simple:

When can we expect returns?

It's a fair question. It's also where expectations frequently break down.

Investors and owners are conditioned to look for immediate progress, visible cost savings, operational improvements, and results that can land in a board pack within the next quarter. AI doesn't get a pass from that pressure. In fact, it often attracts it. The belief is that AI should move faster, deliver sooner, and create value on demand.

Discussion Point: The Real Answer—It Depends

The timeline for AI value capture isn't one-size-fits-all. It depends heavily on how well the organization is prepared to move.

- **Is the organization digitally mature?** Businesses with fragmented systems, manual processes, or poor data hygiene will face longer lead times. Digitally mature organizations can move faster because they have fewer barriers to integration.
- **Are AI resources in place?** If the company already has AI talent, tooling, and a baseline understanding of governance, visible progress will show sooner. If not, building that foundation takes time.
- **Do AI capabilities already exist?** Companies that already have pockets of AI, like lead scoring, chatbots, or demand forecasting, may be able to accelerate value capture by scaling what's already working.
- **Is the leadership aligned?** The speed of execution depends on whether leadership is prepared to preserve the build sequence and prioritize AI initiatives correctly. Misaligned teams will stall, regardless of technical readiness.

The timeline matters, but the real driver is readiness. Some companies can show results in 60 days. Others may take quarters just to stabilize. The answer to "how long do we have to wait" always comes with a qualifier: it depends on how well the business is positioned to move.

The Real Timing: What Can Happen and When

Fast returns are possible, but not all returns are created equal.

- **Within 60–120 days,** secondary system results can show early. These are process improvements, workflow automations, and speed gains that improve reporting, internal efficiency, and operational cadence. These are visible, measurable, and show up quickly.
- **Within 120–180 days, primary** system improvements start to emerge. This is where intelligent capacity begins to build, breaking data silos, enabling cross-functional decision flows, and integrating AI into customer-facing processes. These successes are smaller at first, but start compounding when sequenced correctly.
- **Beyond 180 days:** The more valuable, defensible system-led advantages start to lock in. This is where customer-facing differentiation, structural cost leverage, and intelligent scaling take hold. These results are slower but matter most to buyers and valuation.

Showing positive progress builds confidence, but they don't hold competitive ground forever. Efficiency gets you moving, but it doesn't make you hard to beat. The next step is shifting from internal gains to market-facing advantage, building the kind of differentiation that competitors can't easily copy and buyers are willing to pay for. It's time to move beyond progress and start building what sets the business apart. It's time for differentiation.

Chapter 44

IT'S TIME FOR DIFFERENTIATION

Deciding Where to Point the System's Firepower

The system now has firepower. It can sense live signals, make decisions in motion, and adapt without waiting for manual overrides. But this firepower has to be carefully aimed. Intelligent capacity on its own does not create value. It has to solve real customer problems.

This is the decision point, where to point the system next.

Not every differentiation initiative deserves attention. Some will create customer value that gets noticed, gets used, and earns loyalty. Some will deliver internal wins that look good at status meetings, but do nothing for the customer. The discipline is to focus the system on work that solves meaningful customer problems, shapes pricing power, and creates experiences that customers would actively choose.

Customer value is the filter. If the customer does not feel it, it doesn't matter. If the customer doesn't notice it, it doesn't belong on the list. If the initiative does not solve a real customer problem or make the customer's life meaningfully better, it's a distraction.

When customer problems are solved in a way that feels intelligent, valuable, and hard to copy, it creates differentiation that competitors struggle to match.

How to Pick What Actually Moves the Customer and the Metrics

The system can do more now. That is the problem.

The list of possible initiatives explodes. Everything looks interesting. Everything looks like it could be a win. That is exactly how businesses flood the roadmap with projects that feel urgent but do not actually matter.

This is where prioritization breaks down.

The fastest way to dilute the system's power is to tackle the problems that are easiest to solve but that don't move the needle.

Prioritization shapes structural advantage. The first question always matters:

Does this initiative solve a problem the customer cares about?

The firepower should be aimed at work that:

- Creates pricing flexibility that the customer actually cares about.
- Delivers experiences that feel smarter, faster, and more personalized to the customer in real time.
- Solves friction points that the customer would pay to have removed.
- Accelerates problem resolution in ways that customers can feel, not just track on a dashboard.
- Anticipates customer needs and adjusts product delivery without waiting to be told.
- Unlocks upsell, cross-sell, or expansion paths that feel relevant and timely from the customer's side.

The next question is, does solving that problem move the financial story?

Customer problem solutions that do not shift revenue, retention, margins, or growth may be real, but they do not belong at the front of the system's queue.

Some initiatives will be technically exciting but commercially flat. Some will be financially promising, but solve problems that customers stopped caring about five years ago. The system's firepower should be reserved for the ones that hit both.

The filtering discipline should push hard on three questions:

1. Does the initiative solve a problem the customer would pay to remove?
2. Does the initiative create visible customer impact that strengthens revenue, retention, or pricing power?
3. Does the initiative build intelligent capacity that compounds over time?

If an initiative does not pass the first two, it does not deserve the system's attention. If it passes all three, it's an attractive proposition.

Chapter 45

THE PAYOFF

Turning Intelligent Capacity into Premium Multiples

The work doesn't stop when the system is built. Intelligent capacity sitting idle doesn't create value; it's just an expensive infrastructure. This is where return on investment moves from PowerPoint slides into actual financial results.

The system was never built just to automate tasks or save time. It was built to create a business that thinks faster, adapts smarter, and moves with the market in real-time. And ultimately, to deliver a customer experience that differentiates you from the competition. Now it needs to prove that promise.

What the Payoff Actually Looks Like

When intelligent systems deliver on their promise, the impact shows up across every metric that matters at exit:

Revenue Performance

- Growth accelerates because pricing adapts automatically to market conditions and customer behavior.
- Deal velocity increases because opportunities get surfaced and routed based on real buyer signals.
- Expansion revenue rises because upsell triggers activate based on usage patterns, not calendar schedules.

Margin Expansion

- Gross margins improve because intelligent workflows eliminate bottlenecks without adding headcount.
- Operating leverage increases because the system handles more volume without proportional cost growth.
- Resource efficiency rises because allocation happens in real-time based on demand signals.

Customer Metrics

- Net Revenue Retention climbs because expansion gets triggered by behavioral signals that predict success.
- Gross Revenue Retention stabilizes because the system proactively identifies and protects at-risk accounts.
- Customer satisfaction improves because experiences adapt to individual needs without manual intervention.

Market Position

- Competitive advantage strengthens because intelligent systems create capabilities that are hard to replicate.
- Pricing power increases because value delivery becomes more personalized and defensible.
- Market share grows because the business can respond to opportunities faster than less intelligent competitors.

Why Did We Do This?

Not to create efficiency theater or check AI boxes, but to build compound value that stacks across all dimensions buyers care about. When revenue grows faster, margins expand consistently, and customer metrics strengthen simultaneously, you're not just running a business, you're operating a value creation engine.

The Multiple Impact

Intelligent systems don't just improve individual metrics; they change the financial shape of the business in ways that drive premium valuations:

Predictability: When the system can sense problems early and adapt automatically, financial performance becomes more reliable and projectable.

Scalability: When growth doesn't require proportional increases in complexity or cost, the business becomes more attractive to buyers planning further expansion.

Defensibility: When competitive advantages embedded into system behaviors rather than just processes, they become harder for competitors to copy or buyers to discount.

Optionality: When the system can adapt to new markets, products, or business models, it creates more paths for future value creation.

Beyond the Numbers

The strongest AI-native businesses don't just show better metrics; they demonstrate a different kind of operational capability. They respond to market changes faster, identify opportunities sooner, and execute with less friction and higher confidence.

This operational superiority translates directly into valuation premiums because buyers can see the infrastructure for continued value creation, not just current performance.

When the due diligence team shows up, they don't just see good numbers; they see a business that will keep generating good numbers because it's built to adapt, learn, and improve automatically.

That's the real payoff: not just better performance today, but credible evidence of better performance tomorrow. And in private equity exits, that credibility is what turns good companies into premium acquisitions.

The growth phase is where AI either proves its worth or reveals its limitations. The companies that succeed don't just deploy AI; they build it into the operating model so deeply that removing it would fundamentally change how the business works.

We have argued that intelligent systems only create value when they become the engine behind how the business grows, scales, and adapts. That wasn't philosophy. It was an evidence-backed reality already playing out in deal rooms. The M&A market is sending a clear message: when AI is deeply embedded into the operating model, buyers will pay for it, and sometimes, they'll pay far above sector averages.

Multiples Don't Lie

In a review of over ninety AI-related M&A deals completed in 2025, the average enterprise-value-to-revenue (EV/Revenue) multiple hit 25.8×, more than eight times higher than the median for software companies of similar size and maturity. At the top end, large-language-model vendors commanded 54.8×, and data intelligence platforms weren't far behind at 41.7× (Finro FCA, 2025).

By comparison, the broader private software market from 2015 to mid-2025 delivered a median EV/Revenue multiple of about 3.0×, peaking at 6.0× in early 2021 before cooling to around 2.5×

in mid-2025 (Aventis Advisors, 2025). Top-quartile software deals still rarely breached the 6.4× mark, unless they could demonstrate exceptional performance and defensibility.

The takeaway is stark: AI-native capabilities aren't just improving business metrics, they're reshaping the valuation curve entirely.

Private Equity's Shift in the Playbook

Historically, around 47% of private equity exit returns came from multiple expansion alone (Reuters, 2024). Rising interest rates and reduced re-rating opportunities have changed that math. With market-driven multiple inflation off the table, PE firms are turning to operational transformation, and AI is now a primary lever for creating the profitability and revenue acceleration buyers will pay for.

That shift shows up in diligence. Investors are no longer asking if AI exists in the business; they're asking how it's built into the operating model, how it scales without headcount, and whether its competitive advantages are defensible post-acquisition (Highspring, 2024).

When AI Is the Value Proposition

Consider Smarter Technologies, a healthcare revenue-cycle management platform. Backed by New Mountain Capital, it's part of a rollup strategy integrating AI into every stage of claims processing and payment recovery. The goal is efficiency, and to create a multi-asset platform with embedded intelligence that can process higher volumes with greater accuracy and lower cost. In a healthcare sector where margins are thin and compliance risk is high, that kind of scalable precision becomes a differentiator buyers value at a premium (Business Insider, 2025).

This isn't an isolated case. LLM infrastructure companies acquired in the past year routinely closed at double-digit revenue multiples, not because their code was unique, but because their platforms enabled rapid adaptation across customer bases and verticals, exactly the kind of optionality a strategic acquirer or PE buyer prizes.

Why the Premium Exists

The premiums we see in these transactions align exactly with the drivers outlined earlier:

Predictability — Buyers see more reliable cash flows when AI can detect issues and self-correct before they hit the numbers.

Scalability — Growth without linear cost expansion is visible in the model and the margins.

Defensibility — Capabilities embedded in algorithms and workflows are harder to replicate than process maps or playbooks.

Optionality — Systems that can pivot to new products or markets expand the buyer's future value creation runway.

The Data Behind the Narrative

Call-Out: Exit Multiples That Prove the AI Thesis

Company / Deal	AI Differentiator	Valuation Context
AI M&A deals (90+ across 2025)	Businesses embedding AI across workflows command premium valuation curves—especially health-tech AI.	Average EV/Revenue multiple **25.8×** Development Corporate+6Finro Financial Consulting+6Aventis Advisors+6. Health-tech AI leads with **28.8×** Finro Financial Consulting.
AI Startups (Q2 2025)	Rapid-growth startups (like xAI, Glean) that hit $100M ARR fast are commanding attention—and massive multiples.	Median revenue multiple reached 17.1×, with top performers averaging 50.1× Crowdfund Insider.
Smarter Technologies (New Mountain Capital)	AI-powered revenue cycle platform merging SmarterDx, Thoughtful.ai, and Access Healthcare to streamline hospital billing.	Created via PE consolidation; serves 200+ clients, 60+ health systems, generating over $800M revenue HMP Global Learning NetworkNew Mountain Capital.

Why It Matters

1. **Revenue growth isn't enough**—only when AI is embedded deeply does the market reward it with multiples that dwarf traditional tech benchmarks.

2. **Top-tier AI multiples are real**—with health-tech leading the charge partly because it solves mission-critical, high-cost problems with precision and scale.

3. **Smarter Technologies is the blueprint** for how private equity builds not just functions, but operating-model advantages that buyers can't unbundle.

The conclusion is unavoidable: the market is already rewarding what we've described. Companies that integrate AI into the way they sense, decide, and act are commanding exit valuations that make sector averages look pedestrian.

The Risk of Missing the Moment

The inverse is also true. Companies that treat AI as a feature rather than an operating model are stuck in the averages. In competitive processes, they're not getting penalized because AI doesn't exist — they're getting penalized because the buyer can't see how it will materially change future performance.

Bringing It Back to You

The data reinforces the point: intelligent systems are not theatre, and their payoff is not abstract. The deals are happening now, and the multiples are there for companies that can show real, scalable, defensible AI capability.

In other words: the proof is in the premium. The only question is whether you're building for it, or watching someone else collect it.

The system is ready. The question is whether leadership will use it to build something genuinely differentiated or settle for marginal improvements that disappear under competitive pressure.

The choice determines everything that happens next.

Not every AI initiative lands. Even with the right strategy, governance, and discipline, some builds stall, some assumptions break, and some systems never scale. It's just as important to understand where and why AI efforts fall apart as it is to know what makes them succeed. What happens when it doesn't work, and what to do about it?

Even when the system is working, the pressure doesn't ease. Private equity ownership brings relentless expectations, faster results, tighter reporting, and constant scrutiny. Managing that pressure is part of the job. The next challenge is learning how to keep the system build strategy on track, and the owners engaged, without letting urgency derail the work. This is where discipline meets investor pressure.

References:

Aventis Advisors (2025) Software valuation multiples: 2015–2025 trends.

https://aventis-advisors.com/software-valuation-multiples/?utm_source=chatgpt.com

Business Insider (2025) New Mountain Capital is bringing big exits back to healthcare.

https://www.businessinsider.com/new-mountain-capital-bringing-big-exits-back-healthcare-vc-2025-6?utm_source=chatgpt.com

Crowdfund Insider (2025) AI sector in Q2 2025 sees record M&A, surging valuations, rise of AI agents – research.

https://www.crowdfundinsider.com/2025/08/247085-ai-sector-in-q2-2025-sees-record-ma-surging-valuations-rise-of-ai-agents-research/?utm_source=chatgpt.com

Finro FCA (2025) AI M&A valuation 2025.

https://www.finrofca.com/news/ai-mna-valuation-2025?utm_source=chatgpt.com

Finro FCA (2025) AI revenue multiples 2025.

https://www.finrofca.com/news/ai-revenue-multiples-2025?utm_source=chatgpt.com

Highspring (2024) Enhancing exit readiness: The growing impact of AI and machine learning.

https://www.highspring.com/blog/enhancing-exit-readiness-the-growing-impact-of-ai-and-machine-learning/?utm_source=chatgpt.com

HMP Global Learning Network (2025) Smarter Technologies launches AI-powered revenue cycle management firm following combination of SmarterDx, Thoughtful AI, and Access Healthcare.

https://www.hmpgloballearningnetwork.com/site/ihe/news/smarter-technologies-launches-ai-powered-revenue-cycle-management-firm-following?utm_source=chatgpt.com (Accessed: 11 August 2025).

New Mountain Capital (2025) New Mountain Capital forms Smarter Technologies through combination of SmarterDx, Thoughtful AI, and Access Healthcare.

https://www.newmountaincapital.com/new-mountain-capital-forms-smarter-technologies-through-combination-of-smarterdx-thoughtful-ai-and-access-healthcare/?utm_source=chatgpt.com

Reuters (2024) Buyout barons' dirty secret shows hard times ahead.

https://www.reuters.com/breakingviews/buyout-barons-dirty-secret-shows-hard-times-ahead-2024-09-12/?utm_source=chatgpt.com

Chapter 46

WHEN IT DOESN'T WORK

How Disciplined Failure Builds Stronger Systems

Not every AI project works. In fact, in a private equity timeline where every quarter matters, expecting perfect execution is both unrealistic and counterproductive.

The real mistake isn't failing, it's failing quietly and slowly, dragging initiatives through sprint after sprint while they drain time, trust, and talent.

Why AI Initiatives Fail?

AI fails for the same reasons most change initiatives fail, but the consequences compound faster:

The Problem Wasn't Real: The pain point seemed important in planning sessions, but turned out to be a minor inconvenience that teams could easily work around.

Solution was Built in Isolation: AI was developed without input from the people who needed to use it, creating technically impressive solutions that don't fit actual workflows.

A Data Reality Gap: Models worked beautifully with clean test data but collapsed when fed the messy, incomplete information from production systems.

Organizational Antibodies: The team lost steam when AI required behavior changes that felt like extra work or threatened existing decision-making authority.

None of this is unique to AI, but the risk amplifies because of hype, inexperience, and chronic overestimation of what AI can actually accomplish without serious operational change.

Clear Kill Signals

Stop wasting time on optimization when you should be cutting losses. Five clear signals it's time to shut down an AI project:

1. **No measurable impact after six months** of production deployment.
2. **Declining user adoption** despite training, incentives, and management support.
3. **Manual workarounds consistently deliver better results** than the AI system.
4. **Mounting complexity** that blocks rollout or makes maintenance unsustainable.
5. **Unresolvable dependencies** on data, integrations, or permissions that can't be fixed.

When three or more shows up, you're not optimizing anymore, you're rationalizing a sunk cost.

How to Kill Projects Without Killing Momentum

1. Announce Clearly: Make the decision public. Tell the team, tell the board, be transparent about why the project was stopped. Frame it as disciplined capital allocation, not failure of effort.

2. Harvest the Value: Capture what's still useful, models, workflows, data structures, and technical learnings. Kill the project but keep the pieces worth saving for future initiatives.

3. Run a Rigorous Post-Mortem: Document what failed, what was tried, and what was learned. Be specific. This prevents repeating mistakes and helps other teams launch faster.

4. Redeploy Resources: Move talent, budget, and leadership attention back to high-value work without delay. Let people feel forward movement, not stagnation.

5. Control the Narrative: "We tested. It didn't deliver. Here's what we learned. Here's where we're going next." This isn't retreat, it's operational maturity.

Failure as a Cultural Asset

Strong AI cultures aren't built on perfect execution; they're built on honest failure, fast learning, and transparent review. When teams know they can surface problems early without penalty, they will. When they know failed projects get treated fairly, they'll try again.

Most importantly, when they know the business values learning as much as outcomes, the overall system keeps getting stronger even when individual projects don't work.

Selling Failure at Exit

Here's the counterintuitive truth: disciplined failure strengthens the exit story when positioned correctly.

Buyers aren't expecting flawless track records; they're expecting evidence of smart capital allocation. When the data room includes documentation of killed projects alongside successful ones, it demonstrates:

- Capital discipline under pressure
- Ability to recognize problems and correct the course
- A learning organization that improves over time
- Leadership that makes tough decisions with focus

Frame it right:

Project: AI-powered invoice processing

Goal: Reduce AP processing time by 40%

Outcome: Accuracy plateaued at 62%, adoption declined, and manual processes proved faster

Decision: Shut down after six months, redirected budget to vendor solution that delivered 80% accuracy in 60 days

Learning: Data complexity was underestimated; future projects now require data readiness assessment"

This tells buyers you don't just launch things, you measure, learn, and optimize capital allocation based on results. More importantly, it shows you're willing to kill projects when the data says they aren't delivering. Walking away from underperforming initiatives signals disciplined leadership, not decision-making driven by sunk cost bias or ego. Buyers don't see this as failure; they see it as evidence that resources are defended, priorities are challenged, and capital isn't wasted chasing bad bets.

The Strategic Value of Fast Failure

In PE-backed companies, failed AI projects aren't liabilities if they're handled with discipline. They're proof points that the business knows how to:

- Test hypotheses with clear success criteria
- Allocate capital based on evidence, not hope
- Pivot when reality doesn't match projections
- Learn forward instead of throwing good money after bad

Buyers value this kind of operational maturity. It signals that AI initiatives are managed strategically, not pursued for innovation theater.

The companies that hide failures lose credibility fast. The companies that can demonstrate disciplined failure earn buyer confidence and command premium valuations.

Disciplined execution, smart capital allocation, and the willingness to walk away from the wrong bets all build toward the same goal, unlocking real enterprise value. This is where the system holds, the story holds, and the work pays off. However, there will be an expectation for fast results. Let's examine how to manage that pressure.

Chapter 47

MANAGING PE OWNER PRESSURE

How to Defend the Sequence Without Losing the Room

Private equity owners want fast wins. That is not a secret. The playbook rewards speed, visible savings, and cycle time reduction. The pressure shows up early. It shows up in board meetings, in operating reviews, in quiet side conversations where the question is always the same: what can be delivered this quarter?

That pressure is real. The owners want results now. The problem is when those results start pulling the business off the work that actually creates long-term value.

Defending the sequence while providing owners with something to measure, something to track, and something to report is not resistance for the sake of it. It's discipline that holds the structure together.

The owners are not wrong to want momentum. They are wrong if they believe every margin or EBITDA opportunity should be chased without constraint.

The strongest executives do not fight the pressure. They manage it. Managing pressure also means building the board's conviction to hold the course when the quick wins aren't yet visible. The goal is to make the risks of waiting visible while showing that early action can be taken at a controlled, manageable cost.

Boards rarely back a path because it's visionary; they back it because the first step feels safe and the upside looks disproportionate to the risk. That means:

- Starting with a small, high-probability AI initiative that delivers something tangible in under 90 days.

- Borrowing proof from other industries with similar operating models, even if your sector's AI track record is thin.

- Framing decisions in "probable upside vs. manageable downside" terms, so they look like calculated bets, not leaps of faith.

- Keeping the first move reversible, technically, commercially, and politically, so no one feels locked in if it misfires.

When the board sees traction early, the courage to tackle the bigger changes comes faster. When they see nothing but vision slides, patience evaporates.

Four Moves That Hold the Room

1. Show Early Successes, but Show Them in the Right Lane

The owners need to see that the business is making headway and that it's on track to meet its milestones.

Early successes should be visible, but it should be clear that success is not always financial.

The machine can run. It just needs to run in the right place.

2. Track the Resource Load in Plain Sight

When pressure builds, trade-offs get made in the dark. Resourcing decisions, project approvals, and delivery shifts happen fast when everyone is chasing the next visible win.

The fastest way to manage this is to track where the resources are actually landing. The operating rhythm should show how much capacity is locked on the system build and how much is running secondary system projects.

When that tracking is visible, it gets a seat in the room. When it stays hidden, it gets traded away.

3. Control the Narrative

Owners like speed. They like savings. They like momentum. They also like sequence, but only if someone keeps it in front of them.

The native AI message needs to stay at the top of the story. It's not enough to say it matters. It has to lead the update decks. It has to open the conversations. It has to be the headline.

When financial returns become the headline, the system build starts to fade. As long as the system build stays in the spotlight, the financial wins can show in the background without taking over the room.

Managing the narrative is what holds the discipline in place.

4. Show Them the Future with Data

PE owners aren't just buying the story; they're buying the trajectory. They want to see where the system is headed, not just what it's doing today. The fastest way to manage their pressure is to show them the future, backed by live data.

Forecasts should show when wins will land, when system capacity will unlock, and when measurable impact will hit the financials. AI-driven projections can tighten this view, giving owners forward-looking confidence that helps them stay patient.

But this isn't just about buying time. A well-timed, data-backed pilot creates its own proof point, something owners can touch and measure while the bigger build is underway. Once you give them one credible success, they stop asking "Will it work?" and start asking "Where else can we use it?"

Stay grounded. This is not the time to sell vision, hypotheticals, or distant upside. PE owners don't reward ambition; they reward traction. The future you show has to be data-backed, operationally sound, and tied to clear, visible next steps. Anything else will be dismissed as noise.

Holding the Line Without Losing Support

Managing PE pressure depends on saying yes to the right initiatives, in the right lanes, with the right defenses around the primary system build.

Owners want to see progress. They want to see activity. They want to see savings. Give them that, but make sure they see it, but not at the expense of the system that will create the next round of value.

Managing pressure, delivering wins, and building intelligent capacity are what hold the system together during growth. But growth is only part of the journey. The real payoff comes when the business is ready to step into the exit process with evidence, confidence, and a story that holds under scrutiny. Now, the focus shifts to preparing for an exit, where everything built so far is tested, challenged, and valued.

THE EXIT

Newthistle Consulting LLC

Chapter 48

OPERATOR'S FOREWORD

After many exits, one thing continues to baffle me: the last-minute rush to create an equity story. We have explored the pre-deal, first 100 days, and our transformation journey, but without a clear equity story, i.e. what the next investor's 4–5-year journey looks like, how do we know what we want to build and create?

Few management teams have the capacity (bandwidth) to even consider this, because at the start of their journey, the next investor's equity journey is still 8-10 years away (2 x 4-5 year holds).

Yet in the investment landscape, private equity-backed companies are under increasing pressure to deliver not only strong financial results but also compelling narratives that signal enduring value and future scalability. Nowhere is this more critical than at the point of exit, when value must be crystallized, justified, and clearly articulated to a new generation of investors.

This justification cannot only be something advisors create once we push the exit button. It needs to be the catalyst for the equity strategy and within that, for the AI vision, well before we begin building, engineering, and architecting our AI efforts.

Artificial Intelligence has appeared as a transformative force in the process. No longer a distant frontier, AI is reshaping equity stories and how value creation is evidenced, through areas such as operational efficiency, product enhancement, and strategic differentiation. For businesses preparing for an exit, the thoughtful integration of AI is increasingly becoming a hallmark of readiness, innovation, and resilience.

To enhance the equity story, companies must now go beyond rhetoric and provide tangible evidence of AI-driven impact. This might include demonstrable reductions in customer acquisition costs (CAC) through AI-optimized marketing (enhanced MQLs and SQLs), improved gross margins through predictive support automation, or increased customer retention via intelligent product recommendations (NRR/GRR).

Embedding AI into the core platform of the ecosystem, such as using machine learning for workflow optimization, real-time data and reporting or automation of customer self-service or configuration, can signal a sustainable competitive advantage. Showcasing metrics such as revenue uplift, churn reduction or improved NPS whilst at the same time reducing costs and improving operating margins linked directly to AI initiatives adds credibility to the narrative and creates investor confidence in the scalability of the model.

Whether deployed to optimize internal processes, enhance go-to-market effectiveness, or create predictive analytics within the product, AI is rapidly becoming a core pillar of the equity story.

For the investor community, the question is shifting from whether investors use AI to how AI drives measurable, defensible value and what future potential it unlocks during the holding period.

This chapter offers a roadmap for articulating that value with clarity and conviction. It explores how private equity sponsors and management teams can use AI as both a substance and a signal, how AI can be embedded in the operating model, surfacing its impact on KPIs, and articulating its strategic significance to prospective buyers.

Mark Rogerson – MBE MA MBA

Chapter 49

THE $62 MILLION LESSON

When AI Credibility Collapses Under Buyer Scrutiny

Imagine this. You're five years into a portfolio hold. Revenue growth is steady, EBITDA margins are strong, and a buyer has already floated a nine-figure term sheet. The exit is in sight, and the deck tells a compelling AI-driven growth story, claims of "AI-powered automation" and "proprietary machine learning models" woven through every page.

Then the buyer's technical diligence team starts pulling threads:

- The "proprietary model" turns out to be a lightly tuned, off-the-shelf API anyone can license for $0.002 per query.
- The training data isn't owned, it's scraped from third-party sources with no clear rights.
- Governance documentation? Nonexistent.
- Model drift testing? Never done.

In four days, the AI narrative shifts from "differentiator" to "commodity feature."

In one meeting, the offer drops from $118 million to $56 million.

The buyer's rationale is short and brutal:

> "We're not paying a premium for something anyone can replicate in a week."

The deal still closes. The press release still goes out. But the valuation haircut leaves you explaining to your LPs why almost half the value disappeared in the final lap.

That's the risk in walking into exit with an AI story the buyer can't, or won't, believe. In today's market, they're looking for defensibility, governance, and proof of impact. If they don't find it, they're not negotiating on valuation. They're negotiating on the size of the discount.

The good news? This scenario is avoidable.
Buyers aren't anti-AI, they're anti-hype. They'll pay a premium for AI capabilities that are truly embedded, defensible, and proven to impact revenue, margin, and scalability. The bad news is that most sellers don't know how to package and prove that story before diligence begins.

That's why your AI exit readiness can't be an afterthought. It has to be built and documented from day one of the hold period. The following sections outline exactly what buyers will look for, the pitfalls that trigger discounts, and the steps you can take to position your company for a premium valuation.

Chapter 50

WARNING!

The Test You Should Have Been Preparing For

If you didn't start preparing for due diligence on day one of your private equity journey, you're running late. The diligence process does not reward last-minute scrambling or surface-level fixes. Buyers will find the gaps. They will pull at the threads. They will test whether the system you've built is real, whether the AI story holds, and whether the business can scale without breaking. Preparation is not a phase; it's the way you run the business from the start.

Many years ago, I was a young product manager observing my first due diligence. I sat on the seller's side of the table. Leadership "proudly" displayed a spreadsheet with an extensive list of forecasted contracts for the next 5 years. There was no qualification or justification story. The CEO stood with his arms open as if to say, here it is. The investment lead asked an obvious question, what happens if some or many of those deals do not close? Our executive team's response was, "That is not possible." You can guess what happened to that deal.

The point is that due diligence is not a foregone conclusion. It's hard work, and you need to prepare well in advance.

Chapter 51

WE ARE DIFFERENT!

How to Shift the Diligence Team's Expectations Before the First Question

Many diligence teams will walk into AI-enabled businesses with the wrong mental model. They expect to find AI automating old processes. They are looking for efficiency plays, smoother workflows, and product bolt-ons that make the legacy machine run a little faster and the product look sexier.

They think of AI as a tool that trims cost, simplifies tasks, and improves reporting. Their questions will come from that frame. They will ask how the AI saves time. They will dig into process speed and labor reduction. They will look for system stability, but they will miss the bigger story if you let them.

This is your opportunity to reset their lens before they start.

The way you prepare for technical due diligence should signal from the very beginning that this is not an automation story. This is a system intelligence story. It should show that AI is not wrapped around the edges of the business. It's wired into the core. It does not just improve the system; it changes what the system can do.

You do not need to wait for the diligence Q&A to make this point. The materials you provide, the story you tell, and the way you explain system architecture should all reinforce this difference. You can show that AI is part of the system's learning loop, that it shapes customer experience in real time, and that it's connected to the system's ability to adapt, not just its ability to process.

Your preparation should make it hard for diligence teams to stay stuck in the old inspection playbook. They should see that this is not a company chasing AI as a feature. This is a company that has built AI as a structural capability.

The story should lead with:

- How AI improves decision speed, not just process efficiency.
- How AI shapes customer-facing workflows, not just back-office tasks.
- How AI enables system-level adaptation, not just static reporting.

Show that leadership understands the system's intelligence, not just its ability.

Demonstrate that governance is there to protect learning capacity, not just to limit risk.

When you prepare this way, you set the tone. You make the diligence team ask better questions. You control the frame. You show that this is not just a business with AI, it's a business built for intelligent growth.

That is what changes the conversation. That is what makes buyers lean in.

This is your chance to boast. This is your moment to shout (metaphorically of course). We are different!

- We build systems that adapt, not systems that just run.
- We use AI to reach new markets, not just to move faster in old ones.
- We design intelligence into the core, not as a bolt-on.
- We connect AI to growth, not just to cost.
- We protect the system's ability to learn, not just its ability to comply.
- We can prove the system scales, holds, and earns its way into new spaces.
- We can show that this business is built to grow beyond where it started.

This is the story you want to be heard before diligence begins. This is the hook that lands the fish.

Chapter 52

AI EXIT DUE DILIGENCE

What Sophisticated Buyers Will Examine—And How to Be Ready

If the diligence team has been paying attention, they will have already seen that this is not a process automation story. The way you prepare now needs to show that you can back that story with evidence.

Buyers will not take your word for it. They will test whether the AI actively shapes the way the system thinks, operates, and expands. They will look for proof that AI is not a bolt-on efficiency layer, but a connected, real-time driver of decision-making, customer experience, and market adaptability. They want to see whether the system can stretch into new markets, serve new segments, and scale intelligently without breaking.

Don't fail by claiming system intelligence, then hand over a diligence pack that looks like every other company's process automation story.

Make the connection visible. The system design, governance records, and decision documentation should clearly show:

- How AI is used to improve decision speed, not just task speed.
- How AI interacts with customer-facing workflows, not just back-office reporting.
- How AI outputs are monitored and adjusted in real time, not just in scheduled reviews.

The decision trail must be clean. Buyers will ask why specific AI models were deployed, how those models are monitored, and what decisions were made along the way. They will expect to see those choices captured in architecture diagrams, technical notes, and governance logs. These records should be ready, accessible, and directly linked to customer outcomes.

AI governance is where many companies collapse under diligence. Buyers will not settle for theoretical oversight. They will want to see who owns the models, who approves changes, how risks are tracked, and how system-led decisions are reviewed. They will ask what happens when an AI model drifts, when data changes, or when system recommendations need to be overruled.

Buyers are not just checking whether the system is stable. They are looking for signs that the system can adapt. They will test whether the AI models can learn from new data sources, whether the workflows can support different customer types, and whether the leadership has already thought through how to scale the system into adjacent markets.

What earns their confidence is seeing that the system can handle complexity. Buyers will look for whether AI is being used to explore new pricing strategies, uncover emerging customer needs, or streamline entry into new segments. They want evidence that the system's intelligence is building competitive flexibility, not just operational speed.

Buyers are looking for more than a system that works today. They want to see that the system is designed to unlock future market share.

Data discipline must be visible. Buyers will not just ask where the data comes from. They will test whether the data flows are stable, whether the models depend on fragile pipelines, and whether the system can adjust when data shifts. They will pull hard on this thread.

Technical debt is part of every system, but in AI businesses, hidden debt is dangerous. Buyers will dig to see whether model deployment pipelines are robust, whether explainability has been considered, and whether the system depends on manual patches that leadership has ignored.

The most credible businesses are the ones that run their own internal diligence first. They walk their leadership team through the AI system end-to-end. They test whether the governance processes work in practice, whether the decision trail holds up, and whether the system can be explained without relying on hero developers.

When diligence starts, the story should feel connected with the first question. Buyers should see a system that is intentionally built, intelligently governed, and transparently managed.

They will expect to find gaps. What earns their confidence is whether the leadership knows where those gaps are, whether there is a plan to manage them, and whether the system can grow safely beyond the deal.

This is how you prove you are different. This is how you earn the stretch.

Operator's Log

> *"We were halfway through diligence when the buyer realized the AI system depended entirely on one senior engineer. He was the only one who understood the architecture and the models in production. When that engineer resigned, the buyer walked. That deal taught me a brutal lesson: if knowledge isn't distributed, the system isn't scalable, and the business isn't safe to buy."*
>
> - CTO, Portfolio Company

Preparing for AI exit due diligence builds the foundation, but once buyers enter the room, the focus sharpens. Buyers don't review everything equally; they zero in on specific signals that align with their priorities and risk thresholds. The next step is understanding where buyers actually focus, what questions they'll press hardest, and how to show them the proof they need.

DOWNLOAD: Exit Readiness Ledger
This ledger ensures that companies claiming significant AI capabilities are prepared for the sophisticated due diligence scrutiny they will face from potential buyers. Modern AI due diligence goes far beyond technical validation, it encompasses business validation, financial attribution, legal compliance, and integration readiness.
www.theaifix.online

Chapter 53

BUYER DUE DILIGENCE FOCUS

Turning the AI Narrative into Buyer Confidence

Not all buyers view AI through the same lens. A strategic acquirer, a financial sponsor, and a technical operator will each approach the diligence process with different questions, different priorities, and different definitions of what makes AI valuable.

Understanding these perspectives allows you to tailor the story, the documentation, and the demonstrations to address what each buyer really cares about. The goal is not to deliver a generic AI pitch. The goal is to deliver clear, targeted evidence that builds confidence.

Technology Buyers: Depth, Defensibility, and Scale

Technology buyers, often software platforms and product-led companies, will push deep into the system's technical design. They are not there to see if the AI works. They want to know how it scales, how it integrates, and whether it's built in a way that can support future product expansion.

They will ask:

- Is the system designed for performance under scale?
- Can it flex to support new customer types, geographies, and data sources?
- Can it integrate cleanly into their stack without breaking their existing workflows?

For these buyers, technical defensibility matters. They will probe for proprietary models, algorithms, and data assets that cannot be easily copied. They will assess the system's adaptability, not just its current feature set.

Data quality will come under hard scrutiny. They will test whether the data pipelines are reliable, whether the lineage is clean, and whether the system can absorb new data to enable future market moves.

Technical buyers also evaluate talent risk. They want to see whether AI capability is embedded in the team or whether the system relies on a few key people who may leave. Knowledge retention and well-documented systems are critical.

What helps most:

- Detailed architecture diagrams that show scalability and adaptability.
- Documentation that proves data integrity and system resilience.
- Demonstrations that highlight flexibility, not just process speed.

Strategic Buyers: Impact, Integration, and Growth Pathways

Strategic buyers, often incumbents in specific industries, come looking for growth levers. They want to see whether AI can help them win in their markets, whether it can unlock new customer segments, and whether it can deliver a measurable competitive advantage.

They will ask:

- Has AI driven material outcomes in real-world operations?
- Can this AI capability be integrated across their organization without disruption?
- Can it help them expand their product reach or customer base?

Strategic buyers are especially focused on whether the system can scale horizontally across business units and customer types. They will expect a clear integration roadmap and proof that the AI capabilities will not unravel when exposed to the complexities of their environment.

Regulatory readiness will also be a key checkpoint. Buyers will want to see that governance, model oversight, and compliance are active, not theoretical.

What helps most:

- Case studies showing customer impact and measurable results.
- An integration plan explaining how the system can slot into their operations.
- Clear regulatory documentation and model governance records.

Financial Buyers: Value, Growth, and Risk Exposure

Financial buyers, such as private equity and institutional investors, will focus on value creation and scalability. They will not just ask whether the AI works, they will want to see how it moves EBITDA, how it accelerates growth, and how fast it can scale into new markets.

They will ask:

- How much has AI contributed to revenue, margin, and cost reduction?
- Can those gains be replicated and expanded?
- Does AI unlock new market opportunities or new customer segments?

They will dig into the growth engine. They want to know whether AI multiplies go-to-market efforts, whether it enables cross-selling, and whether it creates financial headroom to scale efficiently.

Risk management is a major focus. Financial buyers will look for operational, technical, and compliance risks, as well as concentration risk if key AI systems depend on external vendors or fragile data sources.

What helps most:

- Clean, auditable financial data that ties AI to business impact.
- Growth plans that show clear pathways to market expansion.
- A comprehensive risk register that addresses technical, operational, and regulatory exposures.

Unifying Theme: Confidence Across Buyer Types

By the time diligence starts, the conversation is about confidence.

- **Technical buyers** want confidence that the system will scale.
- **Strategic buyers** want confidence that the system will integrate and grow their market position.
- **Financial buyers** want confidence that the system will sustain and multiply value.

Each buyer is chasing something different: technical resilience, market reach, or financial upside, but all are looking for the same signal,

Is this real, or is it a well-polished illusion?

If your answers do not meet their expectations, the valuation drops.

Prepare accordingly. Align the story, back it with evidence, and deliver with precision, because buyer confidence is what gets deals done at premium multiples.

Operator's Log

> *"We told a flat, generic AI story to every buyer. We didn't adjust. The technology buyer wanted to understand scale and data flow. The strategic buyer wanted market integration and product fit. The financial buyer wanted growth levers and proof of margin expansion. We gave them all the same slide deck. They all passed. One-size storytelling cost us the deal."*
>
> \- Portfolio Company CEO

Buyer focus is rarely smooth, and the exit process is never clean. It's a high-pressure gauntlet of competing demands, parallel diligence streams, and shifting buyer expectations. Preparing is one thing; navigating it in real time is another. The next step is learning how to hold the story, align the leadership team, and manage the chaos as the process moves. This is where exits are either defended or quietly dismantled.

Chapter 54

SELLING COMPOUNDING VALUE

Shifting the Exit Narrative from Risk to Return

When it's time to exit, governance and documentation matter, but what wins buyers over isn't just policy binders and risk logs. It's seeing a system that compounds value without needing reinvention.

Plenty of companies can prove they've "used AI." Fewer can show that the business *runs* on it. Fewer still can show that the system gets smarter with scale, adapts with less effort, and produces results that don't fade with leadership changes or market shifts.

Buyers want a machine that keeps working after the founders leave.

What to Prove:

1. The System Owns the Process

You're not just selling dashboards or AI features. You're selling workflows that adjust in real time, reroute based on live feedback, and evolve without manual intervention.

Example: Lead scoring isn't a spreadsheet or a static formula; it's a continuously improving engine that tracks signal-to-conversion accuracy and retrains itself based on performance. That's not a feature. It's IP.

2. Compounding, Not Churn

Show that value creation continues even as people change. You don't need to keep expensive talent in place to keep the flywheel turning.

Example: A team change didn't require a full re-onboarding of your sales process, because the routing logic, customer signals, and outreach behaviors are owned by the system, not tribal knowledge.

3. Governance Is a Capability, Not a Safety Net

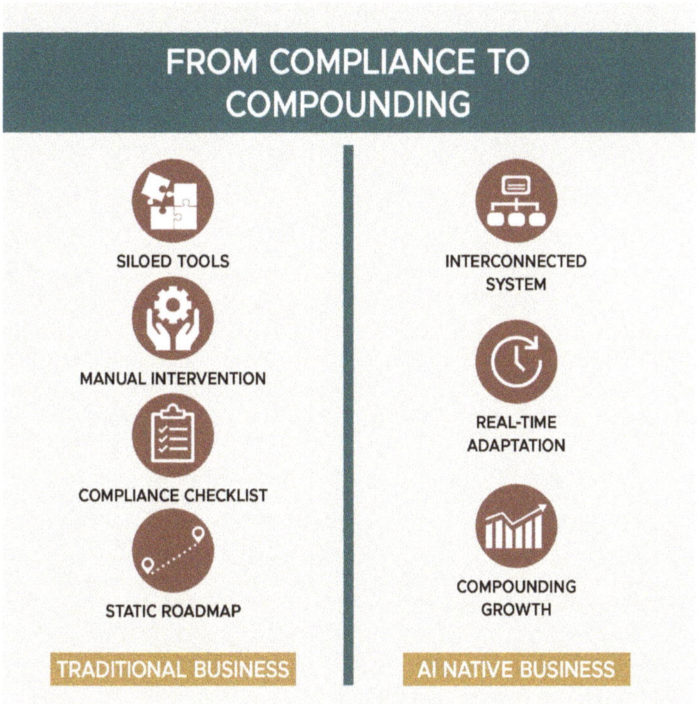

Buyers want to know they're not inheriting hidden liabilities. But more than that, they want to see that governance isn't a band aid, it's embedded into how AI gets deployed, updated, and monitored.

Example: Every AI decision in your system logs its source model, decision context, and confidence threshold. It doesn't need a retroactive explanation; it's already explainable.

4. Scalable Without Redesign

Show that new teams, new markets, and new use cases integrate into the system without re-architecture.

Example: You added a new product line in Q2. It plugged directly into the same data foundation, signal pipelines, and automation scaffolding already in place. No new rebuild. Just expansion.

Exit Positioning: What Buyers Actually Hear

Don't say:

"We've embedded AI in our workflows and documented the governance."

Do say:

"This is an intelligent system that senses, decides, and adapts on its own. It's already delivering measurable gains, and it scales without reinvention. You're not buying a tech debt pile, you're buying a system that compounds."

That's the difference between selling an asset with tech exposure... and commanding a premium for an asset with *system leverage*.

Chapter 55

NAVIGATING THE EXIT GAUNTLET

Due Diligence Pitfalls and How to Avoid Them

Even with the excitement around AI-enhanced businesses, most due diligence efforts fall into familiar traps, some technical, others organizational. These aren't theoretical problems; they show up in real-world transactions as delays, valuation discounts, and post-close surprises. In this chapter, we walk through the most common pitfalls investors encounter when evaluating AI companies and how to avoid them. The goal is not just risk mitigation, but smarter decision-making and higher confidence during the diligence process.

The exit process is not clean. It's a collision of diligence streams, competing buyer agendas, and parallel questions that can pull leadership in different directions. Preparation gets you to the start line, but managing the exit as it unfolds is its own discipline.

When the process moves, the story must hold. The leadership team must stay aligned. The evidence must be consistent. The AI narrative must not drift.

This is where exits start to wobble.

Leadership Alignment Under Pressure

During diligence, multiple buyer teams will ask similar questions in different ways, often at the same time. One team might focus on system architecture. Another might probe financial drivers. A third might push on governance.

The risk is that leadership answers drift. Sales say AI drives margin. Operations say AI drives speed. Finance says AI supports cost reduction. The buyers will notice.

Managing the exit means aligning the leadership team to one story and one set of proof points.

People Preparation and Points of Failure

The leadership team does not just need to know the story; they each need to own part of it.

Buyers will test whether the system depends on a single architect, a single developer, or a single executive who carries the knowledge. They will probe to see if the system can survive leadership turnover, team transitions, or technical handoffs.

One of the most damaging signals during an exit is the appearance of a single point of failure.

If every detailed answer runs through the CTO.

If AI model oversight only sits with one lead developer.

If governance records live in one person's inbox.

Buyers will spot it, and confidence will crack.

Who Prepares for What?

- **CEO:** Must be able to speak fluently about the system's role in growth, scalability, and customer impact. Cannot defer all system questions to the technical team.
- **CFO:** Must understand how AI contributes to financial performance, where the AI-related risks sit, and how system growth ties to margin and cash flow. Cannot treat AI as a black box.
- **CTO/Technology Lead:** Must own the system architecture story, model governance, scalability pathways, and technical debt management. Cannot act as the sole source of truth.
- **Product/Operations Leader:** Must be able to show how AI integrates into customer workflows and how the system adapts to different customer needs. They cannot pass all AI-related questions to engineering.
- **Data Lead:** Must own the explanation of data pipelines, data governance, and model monitoring. Buyers will expect detailed answers here.

The Primary Rule: No Single Thread

Every buyer interaction should reinforce that the system's knowledge is shared, documented, and distributed.

If one leader steps out of the room, the answers continue.

If one team lead leaves the business post-transaction, the system holds.

Buyers are not just buying technology. They are buying continuity.

If the business looks like it will unravel when one person walks out the door, the deal will soften.

Avoid the impression of dependency. Build depth across the team. Train successors. Document decisions. Share system ownership.

This makes the business look safe to buy.

This delivers the value at the table.

Everyone should be able to answer:

- Where AI drives impact.
- How AI is embedded in the system.
- How the system adapts and scales.

Consistency matters more than polish. Buyers will forgive imperfect answers, but they will rarely forgive conflicting ones.

Managing Information Flow

Buyers will often run concurrent diligence streams across technical, financial, and commercial tracks. They will ask for the same data points in different contexts.

The danger is in over-disclosing, duplicating answers, or providing inconsistent details to different teams.

Managing the exit means controlling the information flow.

- Track what has been provided, to whom, and when.
- Keep a single source of truth for AI-related answers and documentation.
- Assign a coordination lead to manage cross-stream

communication.

The right hand must always know what the left hand is saying.

Handling AI Demonstrations

Buyers will often ask to see the AI in action. This is where many exits fall apart. Teams overextend themselves, run demos that are too complex, or show in-development features that can't yet hold up in production.

The safest path is to show:

- Live demonstrations of real, production-ready workflows.
- Clear examples of AI supporting decision velocity or market adaptability.
- Controlled use cases that tie directly to the business impact already discussed.

Do not show unfinished features. Do not improvise. Do not over-promise.

Buyers are not expecting perfection. They are looking for operational confidence. Show what works. Be precise about what is still evolving.

Managing Buyer Personas Without Shifting the Story

Different buyers will want to pull the AI narrative in different directions.

- Technical buyers will push on architecture and scalability.
- Strategic buyers will push on integration and growth pathways.
- Financial buyers will push on revenue and risk.

There is a temptation to reshape the story to suit each buyer's angle. That is a mistake.

The story does not shift. The emphasis shifts.

Each buyer gets a version of the same system story, consistently told, consistently evidenced. The framing may highlight different benefits, but the system's core design, governance, and scalability story does not change.

If the story shifts under pressure, confidence drops, and value erodes.

Final Discipline: Holding the Story

Managing the exit well means consistent storytelling all the way through:

- Align leadership to one story and one proof set.
- Control what is shared, when, and with whom.
- Show only what is ready and production-proven.
- Stay disciplined when buyers probe from different angles.

The businesses that hold the story under pressure are the ones that stretch multiples.

The exit hinges on more than what you built. It depends on how well you hold the story together when everyone else is trying to tear it apart.

Operator's Log

> *"During live diligence, our CEO told the buyer the system was fully proven at scale. I told them the scalability was still in progress. That inconsistency cut our credibility in half, and it cut the valuation by 20% overnight. I learned that alignment comes from leadership consistently speaking the same truth to every buyer, not from rehearsing perfect answers."*
>
> \- Portfolio Company CTO

Even when the deal is moving, it's not finished. Pre-deal close is where unresolved issues surface, final terms tighten, and last-minute negotiations can either hold value or erode it. This is the stage where leadership must actively close the gaps, manage buyer concerns, and protect the deal from slipping. The next step is navigating pre-deal close resolution, the final pressure test before the finish line.

Chapter 56

PREMIUM v DISCOUNTED EXITS

What Buyers Really Pay For

AI can boost multiples or burn them.

In today's deal environment, simply having "AI" in the pitch deck won't drive a premium. Buyers are no longer paying for promise. They're paying for proof. The difference between a premium and a discounted exit often comes down to one question: Can the acquirer scale it, trust it, and defend it?

Think back to the $62 million haircut scenario. That deal didn't crater because the market turned or the buyer got cold feet. It cratered because the AI claims collapsed under inspection. Everything else in the business was strong, but the premium was built on a foundation the buyer didn't believe. That's the difference between a premium exit and a discounted one.

This chapter breaks down what buyers are actually looking for when they value AI in an exit process. It shows how strategic integration, operational lift, and defensible IP drive premium outcomes, while cosmetic, bolt-on AI features invite scrutiny and discounting.

Two case studies illustrate the spread:

- One business embedded AI as a core infrastructure and earned a premium.
- The other led with buzzwords and paid the price.

Understanding that difference is what separates exit stories that command attention from those that fall apart under due diligence.

Case Study: Industrial Automation Company (Premium Exit)

Background:

A PE-backed industrial automation company spent three years embedding AI into its manufacturing operations.

AI Capabilities:

- Developed proprietary AI algorithms for production scheduling and predictive maintenance.
- Integrated a real-time analytics platform across all plants.
- Built up five years of operational data, creating a defensible data moat.

Exit Process:

- Technical due diligence highlighted the "plug-and-play scalability" of the AI platform.
- Strategic acquirers valued the AI core as a foundation for scaling intelligent automation across their own operations.

Outcome:

- **Valuation:** Achieved 14.2x EBITDA, compared to an industry median of 12.3x.
- **Premium Justification:** The acquirer cited the AI core as the main driver for the premium, emphasizing its defensibility and scalability.
- **Narrative:** The exit story focused on quantifiable AI-driven margin expansion, operational resilience, and future scalability.

Case Study: SaaS Platform with Superficial AI (Discounted Exit)

Background:

A SaaS company marketed itself as "AI-powered," but its capabilities were limited to off-the-shelf chatbots and basic analytics.

AI Capabilities:

- AI use was confined to customer support automation and simple reporting.
- No proprietary models or integrated learning systems.
- Data infrastructure was fragmented, and most workflows remained manual.

Exit Process:

- Technical due diligence revealed that AI features accounted for less than 10% of platform usage.

- Most "AI" was vendor-supplied, with no defensible differentiation.

Outcome:

- **Valuation:** Exited at 8.5x EBITDA, below the sector median of 10x.
- **Discount Reason:** The buyer applied a discount due to lack of proprietary IP, weak integration, and no evidence of AI-driven customer retention or margin improvement.
- **Narrative:** The exit story could not credibly link AI to business outcomes, resulting in skepticism and a lower offer.

Comparative Table: Premium vs. Discounted AI Exits

DIMENSION	PREMIUM EXIT (INDUSTRIAL AUTOMATION)	DISCOUNTED EXIT (SAAS PLATFORM)
AI Integration	Core, proprietary, systemwide	Superficial, vendor-supplied
Due Diligence	Highlighted as key differentiator	Revealed lack of substance
Valuation Multiple	14.2x EBITDA (15% premium)	8.5x EBITDA (discounted)
Buyer Rationale	Scalable, defensible AI advantage	No moat, easily replicable features
Exit Narrative	Quantifiable, defensible, future-ready	Non-credible, failed to convince buyers

Key Takeaways

- A **premium exit** is achieved when AI is deeply embedded, creating measurable, defensible advantages that buyers can scale.
- **Discounted exits** result from cosmetic or poorly integrated AI,

unsupported by operational and financial evidence.

- The exit story must be credible, quantified, and clearly linked to business outcomes buyers care about.

By understanding these dynamics, PE operators can build and position AI capabilities that command higher multiples and withstand the scrutiny of sophisticated buyers.

This chapter showed what separates a premium exit from a discounted one. It isn't hype. It's not AI as decoration. Premium outcomes are earned when intelligent systems are embedded deeply enough to drive margin, scalability, and defensibility that buyers can validate.

But the story doesn't end with the exit.

For the next generation of companies, that kind of value creation isn't optional. It's the baseline.

We now move beyond the deal lifecycle and into the new strategic reality: a business environment reshaped by AI, compressed decision cycles, and systems that won't slow down to wait for leaders still making sense of the last quarter.

This next chapter is a warning and a window.

Because while you've been planning your roadmap, the future has been rewriting the rules.

Chapter 57

AI NARRATIVE CONSTRUCTION

Building Compelling Stories That Command Premium Valuations

In private equity exits, technical excellence does not close the deal. Compelling stories do. The best AI exits show what AI technology delivers, but more importantly, they tell a story that buyers believe, a story about sustainable advantages, expanding markets, and transformational growth.

A good narrative can add millions to your valuation. A weak one can quietly erase them, fast. We've already seen how quickly a nine-figure term sheet can slide when the buyer decides your AI advantage is cosmetic. The haircut wasn't about poor storytelling, it was about a story that couldn't survive technical diligence.

This chapter shows how to build an AI narrative that holds under diligence, resonates with different buyer types, and drives valuation.

The Core Structure of a Winning Narrative

1. The Business Problem (The "Why")

Every strong narrative starts with a real problem. Without it, AI is just a shiny tool.

Buyers want to hear:

- A specific, high-impact business problem worth solving.
- Quantified pain, revenue at risk, costs to eliminate, markets to capture.
- Evidence that the problem matters to real customers, right now.

If the problem is weak, the story falls apart. If it's urgent and undeniable, buyers lean in.

2. The AI Solution (The "What")

Once the problem is nailed, the solution must be clear, differentiated, and provable.

Buyers will ask:

- What exactly does the AI do?
- How is it built, and why is it better than alternatives?
- Where is it integrated into the system, not just as a feature, but as a capability?

Generic AI does not move multiples. Integrated, defensible, system-level intelligence does.

3. The Business Impact (The "So What")

Technology is not enough. Buyers want to see the impact.

The narrative must connect:

- AI capabilities to revenue, retention, and market growth.
- Quantified business outcomes, clear financial results.
- Real customer adoption and operational performance.

The best AI exits prove the link between what the system does and what the business earns.

4. The Future Opportunity (The "What's Next")

The story must show buyers where this can go.

Buyers will look for:

- Clear pathways to expand into new markets or product lines.
- A technology roadmap that supports future growth.
- A credible vision that is bold, but not fantasy.

What buyers really want is the option to grow beyond what exists today. The narrative should make that future look not just possible, but inevitable.

Example Technology Buyer Narrative: *"Customer behavior analytics are evolving from descriptive reporting to predictive intelligence. Our proprietary behavioral AI, trained on 500M+ customer interactions, predicts purchasing intent with 94% accuracy, 3x better than rule-based systems. This dataset becomes more valuable with scale, creating a defensible moat. Integration with the platform extends AI capabilities to over 10,000 customers immediately, while the existing team accelerates AI development across product lines.*

Example Strategic Buyer Narrative: *"Healthcare providers face mounting pressure to improve outcomes while reducing costs. Our AI diagnostic platform, deployed across 200+ facilities, reduces diagnostic errors by 40% and cuts imaging interpretation time by 60%. Health systems report $2M+ annual savings per facility while achieving better patient outcomes. Integration across your 500+ facilities will create the industry's largest AI-powered diagnostic network, positioning you as the clear market leader in AI-driven healthcare."*

Example Financial Buyer Narrative: *"Manufacturing automation represents a $50B+ market growing 25% annually as labor costs rise and efficiency demands increase. Our AI-powered predictive maintenance platform generates average EBITDA improvements of 35% across 150+ manufacturing facilities, with a documented ROI of 400%+ within 18 months. The platform scales efficiently, and adding new facilities requires minimal incremental investment while expanding our data advantage. With 100,000+ potential facilities in our addressable market and clear expansion into adjacent AI applications, we project 3x revenue growth over five years. Strategic buyers in industrial automation consistently pay 15-20x EBITDA for proven AI platforms, positioning this investment for exceptional exit returns."*

Tailoring the AI Narrative by Buyer Type

While the core story stays constant, different buyers look for different signals. The narrative must flex to meet those expectations without shifting the foundation.

For Technology Buyers

What they want: System resilience, scalability, and technical defensibility.

What to emphasize:

- Detailed system design and how AI is integrated into the core.
- Scalability across data volumes, geographies, and customer types.

- Proprietary models, protected data assets, or unique system intelligence.

What they will challenge:

- Model fragility, brittle pipelines, and technical debt.
- Whether the AI is really differentiating or just chasing feature parity.

The story should show that the system scales without breaking and that the technology is not easily replicated.

For Strategic Buyers

What they want: Market expansion, customer growth, and rapid integration.

What to emphasize:

- How AI enables entry into new segments or enhances competitive positioning.
- Demonstrated customer adoption and measurable impact.
- Integration pathways into the buyer's existing products or operations.

What they will challenge:

- Whether AI performance can be replicated at scale inside their business.
- Whether the system can support their regulatory and operational constraints.

The story should make integration look smooth, market expansion look achievable, and revenue growth look sustainable.

For Financial Buyers

What they want: Margin expansion, scalable growth, and manageable risk.

What to emphasize:

- Financial performance directly tied to AI-driven improvements.
- Operating leverage enabled by the system's intelligence.
- Visibility into risks, governance, and technical debt.

What they will challenge:

- Whether the growth story is already priced in.
- Whether key AI claims can hold up under scaled execution.

The story should make the growth playbook look repeatable, the system look de-risked, and the financial upside look achievable.

Final Alignment

The core system story does not shift.

What changes are the framing, the emphasis, and the proof points.

- **Technology buyers** need to hear that the system is built to scale.
- **Strategic buyers** need to hear that the system can accelerate their growth.
- **Financial buyers** need to hear that the system drives returns and holds value.

Staying Aligned

The strongest exits deliver one system story with carefully adjusted focus areas for each buyer type. The story does not drift. The narrative flexes to meet each buyer's lens, but the foundation, the system design, the governance, and the customer impact, remains consistent.

- Technology buyers need to see system depth.
- Strategic buyers need to see market reach.
- Financial buyers need to see scalable value.

When each buyer finds the proof, they need in a story that holds steady across the process. That's when the deal builds momentum. That's when buyers start to see the real opportunity and when the deal moves from consideration to pursuit.

Operator's Log

> *"We had strong technology, but the story fell apart in diligence. The CEO emphasized customer impact. The product lead focused on automation. The finance team couldn't link AI to the financial model. The buyer's team caught the gaps immediately. We didn't lose because the system failed, we lost because the story didn't hold. A fractured narrative is a dead narrative."*
>
> \- Operating Partner, Technology-Focused PE Fund

A strong narrative can carry the deal. A weak one can quietly unravel it. Even solid businesses lose momentum when the story breaks down, drifts, or misses what buyers care about most. The next step is knowing where AI narratives fail and how to avoid the mistakes that erode credibility, confidence, and value. These are the narrative pitfalls to avoid.

Chapter 58

AI IN THE EQUITY STORY

Proof, Not Promise

When it comes to preparing for exit, every portfolio company has a story to tell. In the AI era, that story is often framed around transformation, differentiation, and a future-proof business model. But while it's easy to talk about "baking AI into the narrative," buyers and their diligence teams are not swayed by buzzwords, they want proof.

The equity story must be underpinned by verifiable performance, customer adoption, and operational impact. Done well, AI can be the lever that drives valuation multiples beyond the market norm. Done poorly, it can unravel the deal entirely.

Case Study 1: AI-Enabled Revenue as a Valuation Multiplier

New Mountain Capital's HealthTech Rollup – Smarter Technologies

In 2025, New Mountain Capital created Smarter Technologies by combining Access Healthcare with two high-growth AI firms, SmarterDx and Thoughtful AI. The new entity leveraged AI to optimize revenue cycle management in hospitals and health systems, using machine intelligence to identify claim errors, accelerate reimbursements, and cut administrative costs.

The impact was more than operational efficiency, it fundamentally changed the revenue model. By embedding AI-driven automation and analytics into recurring service contracts, Smarter Technologies built predictable, sticky revenue streams in a sector where switching costs are high.

The result was a narrative that was both defensible and compelling: a mature healthcare operator with proven AI infrastructure, capable of compounding margins and scaling into adjacent services. In a market still hungry for AI-backed operational plays, this positioned the asset for a premium valuation at exit (Business Insider, 2025).

Case Study 2: When the AI Narrative Collapsed Under Diligence

Builder.ai – The AI Washing Disaster

Not all AI equity stories survive contact with a buyer's diligence team. Builder.ai, once hailed as a UK unicorn and backed by Microsoft, promised a generative AI platform that could build custom apps "like ordering pizza." Behind the scenes, however, the core delivery relied on hundreds of human developers rather than autonomous AI.

Worse, internal documents later revealed revenue inflation of up to 300%, a red flag that triggered investor and buyer withdrawals. When these facts emerged, the AI narrative collapsed overnight, leading to insolvency in 2025. The company's reputation, and any potential premium exit, was destroyed (Vaultinum, 2025; TechInformed, 2025).

Premium vs Discounted Exit – AI in the Equity Story

Premium Exit – Smarter Technologies	Discounted/Failed Exit – Builder.ai
PE Owner: New Mountain Capital	**VC-Backed:** Microsoft, others
AI Role: Embedded in revenue cycle management, automating claim validation and reimbursement	**AI Role:** Marketed as an AI-powered app builder but reliant on large teams of human developers
Revenue Model: Recurring, contract-based services with high switching costs	**Revenue Model:** Project-based, low switching costs, overinflated revenue reporting
Proof Points: Documented operational impact, measurable margin gains, defensible technology	**Proof Points:** Unverified claims, no audited AI performance data
Defensibility: Proprietary processes + embedded AI make replication difficult	**Defensibility:** Low—model could be replicated or replaced
Buyer Perception: AI story matched by operational data and recurring revenue streams	**Buyer Perception:** Narrative collapsed under due diligence
Valuation Impact: Premium multiple driven by AI-enabled growth and stickiness	**Valuation Impact:** Collapse of deal, insolvency in 2025
Exit Lesson: Build the AI equity story years before exit with real, audit-proof results	**Exit Lesson:** Marketing spin without verifiable results destroys trust and value

The cautionary lesson is stark: unverified AI claims, once exposed, don't just weaken a story, they can obliterate value. In Builder.ai's case, "AI-enabled" became shorthand for overpromise and underdeliver.

Why This Matters for PE Operators

Both stories contain the same core truth: AI is only as valuable as the proof that underpins it. Smarter Technologies used AI to create recurring, contractually protected revenue streams and operational leverage, tangible drivers of valuation multiples. Builder.ai relied on perception, not proof, and collapsed when the perception was challenged.

In the exit phase, "AI-enabled" must mean more than marketing language. It must translate into:

- **Quantifiable impact** on revenue quality, margin expansion, or customer retention.
- **Defensible differentiation** that competitors can't easily replicate.
- **Operational evidence** that stands up to deep technical and commercial diligence.

For portfolio companies, this means starting the AI equity story long before the exit process begins, building the capabilities, embedding them in customer contracts, and documenting results in a way that buyers can audit without hesitation.

Premium multiples aren't just a product of what your business is, they're also a product of how that story is told and defended when the buyer is in the room. The right numbers can still lose their punch if the narrative is generic, the proof is thin, or the delivery misses the mark. That's where deals quietly bleed value. In the next chapter, we'll strip out the theory and get blunt about the most common misfires that sink otherwise strong exits, and how to make sure yours isn't one of them.

References

Business Insider (2025) *New Mountain Capital Is Bringing Big Exits Back to Healthcare.*

https://www.businessinsider.com/new-mountain-capital-bringing-big-exits-back-healthcare-vc-2025-6

Vaultinum (2025) *AI-Washing: Lessons from the Builder.ai Collapse.*

https://vaultinum.com/blog/ai-washing-lessons-from-the-builder-ai-collapse

TechInformed (2025) *Unicorn Builder.ai Collapses Amid Inflated Revenue Claims and FOMO Investing.*

https://techinformed.com/unicorn-builder-ai-collapses-amid-inflated-revenue-claims-and-fomo-investing/

Chapter 59

NARRATIVE PITFALLS TO AVOID

How to Lose Credibility—and the Deal—Before Reaching the Finish Line

Every exit has two stories running in parallel: the one you want to tell, and the one the buyer is actually listening for. The gap between them is where value disappears. You can have the best numbers in the room and still lose leverage if the narrative doesn't align with the buyer's priorities, if it collapses under basic scrutiny, or if it's so generic it could apply to half the companies in your sector.

The market doesn't reward "almost." Almost compelling, almost convincing, almost defensible, these are the warning lights on the dashboard of a deal that's about to underperform. Buyers walk away with the price they're willing to pay, not the one you think you've earned.

Here, we strip away the comfortable illusions, because even technically solid, factually accurate stories can backfire if they're framed poorly, aimed at the wrong target, or delivered without discipline. The goal is to avoid the obvious blunders, and to recognize how seemingly small missteps in positioning, proof, or delivery can knock points off your multiple before you even realize it's happening.

The Six Pitfalls of Storytelling

Generic Storylines

Telling the same story to every buyer is a shortcut to irrelevance. Different buyers value different things, leverage, market growth, scalability, and a one-size pitch lands with none of them.

Protect yourself: Tailor the narrative to the buyer's lens. Show you understand what drives their valuation model.

Tech-First Framing

Opening with models, features, and architecture excites engineers, but most buyers hear "cost center."

Protect yourself: Lead with business impact. Let the tech prove the point, not steal the spotlight.

Vision Without Traction

Pitching the future without showing present momentum makes your story sound speculative.

Protect yourself: Anchor in what's already working. Treat future upside as bonus, not the main event.

Inconsistent Messaging

When leadership tells different versions of the story, buyers see confusion or misdirection, both kill confidence.

Protect yourself: Align the team on a single, evidence-backed narrative. Rehearse until it's bulletproof.

Weak Evidence

Claims without proof are exit poison. Buyers expect adoption data, operational metrics, and financial outcomes, not vague assertions.

Protect yourself: Build your evidence pack early. Back every claim with data you can defend in diligence.

Boring or Overcomplicated Delivery

A strong business can still sound like a risky bet if the pitch is wrapped in jargon or drains the room's energy.

Protect yourself: Keep it clear, keep it engaging. Buyers remember what's easy to follow and hard to forget.

Final Watch Point

Narratives fall apart when they drift from what's real, when they ignore the buyer's priorities, or when they collapse under their own complexity.

The best exits don't just tell a good story. They tell the right story, the one that holds up under scrutiny, that matches what the system can prove, and that meets the buyer where they are.

The companies commanding premium multiples in today's market aren't just the ones with superior systems, they're the ones that can prove it in a way that lands with buyers. Every misfire above erodes that proof, chipping away at the credibility that turns strong performance into valuation leverage. The data in the last chapter shows the upside when the story, the system, and the evidence line up. This section is about making sure you don't fumble that advantage in the final mile. In an exit, you only get one room, one shot, and one number. Protect it.

Operator's Log

> *"We had the technical metrics and financial impact data, but our initial exit narrative was boring and tactical. 'Our AI improves efficiency by 20%', so what? We completely reimagined the story around market transformation: 'We're the only company that's proven AI eliminates manual insurance claims processing while improving accuracy. In a $500B industry where everyone talks about AI, we're the only ones who've deployed it at scale.' Same technology, completely different narrative. Went from 8x EBITDA offers to 15x EBITDA with a bidding war."*
>
> — CEO, Insurance Technology Portfolio Company

Chapter 60

PROBLEM RESOLUTION

How to Land the Deal Without Eroding Value

Due diligence doesn't end when the last question is answered. It carries forward, shaping the final negotiation, the pricing adjustments, and the risk protections that buyers demand before the deal can close.

This is the phase where gaps must be resolved, not ignored. What's uncovered in diligence doesn't fade into the background. It becomes the foundation for the final deal terms.

Real Work in Pre-Deal Resolution

The critical work in this phase is to address buyer concerns with speed, structure, and credibility. Buyers need to see that leadership isn't scrambling or sidestepping. They need to see mature, documented plans that resolve open issues.

What Must Be Resolved?

- **AI Performance Gaps**: If models aren't performing as promised, present a remediation timeline, retraining plans, or system adjustments with clear owners and measurable checkpoints. Buyers will not accept vague commitments.

- **Data Quality Concerns:** If diligence exposes weak data pipelines or inconsistent lineage, show a proactive investment in data governance. Buyers will push for visible fixes and sometimes third-party audits to verify the improvements.

- **Integration Friction:** When system architecture raises questions, buyers will expect revised integration plans, possibly including alternative deployment strategies or architectural upgrades. Show that the system will not break post-close.

- **Security and Compliance Gaps:** Any weaknesses will trigger scrutiny. Be prepared to deliver remediation documentation, updated controls, and possibly independent certifications to settle these concerns.

Commercial Resolution Points

- **ROI Credibility:** Buyers will challenge any numbers that feel optimistic or poorly substantiated. Be ready to provide deeper analysis, operational proof, or external validation to hold the valuation line.
- **Customer Adoption and Satisfaction:** If usage rates or satisfaction scores are lower than expected, present customer re-engagement plans, feedback loops, and evidence that the system is already improving.
- **Market Positioning Weaknesses:** If diligence reveals a diluted competitive narrative, update positioning materials and articulate a clearer go-to-market strategy that buyers can carry forward.
- **Regulatory Readiness:** Especially in sensitive industries, unresolved compliance risks will stall deals. Provide clear, documented plans that show how these gaps will close, and when.

Deal Structure Implications

If issues are unresolved, buyers will shield themselves.

- **Valuation Adjustments:** Buyers may apply price reductions, holdbacks, or earn-outs tied to the completion of technical fixes or performance milestones.
- **Risk Protections:** Buyers may require indemnifications, escrow arrangements, AI-specific insurance, or post-close reporting obligations to manage unresolved risks.
- **Transition Support:** Buyers will often negotiate structured knowledge transfer, leadership continuity, and post-close technical support to prevent value leakage.

What This Phase Signals

The pre-close resolution phase signals whether the leadership team is mature, disciplined, and capable of navigating real scrutiny. Show that the company can operate under pressure and finish what it starts.

Buyers expect to find gaps. What they don't expect is a leadership team that has already mapped the fixes, already assigned owners, and already built the pathways to close those gaps with precision.

That's how trust is preserved. That's how value is defended.

This is where the deal either accelerates or drags toward erosion.

Sellers who face issues head-on and close them decisively will protect the multiple. Those who delay or deflect will watch the deal bleed value.

In the end, pre-close resolution isn't just the clean-up. It's the final proof of discipline. It's the last signal buyers see before they write the check.

Operator's Log

> *"We thought we were ready for technical due diligence with our basic AI documentation. The buyer brought in a team of ML engineers who spent three weeks testing our models, auditing our data pipelines, and stress-testing our systems. They found performance inconsistencies we didn't know existed and data quality issues that required six months to fix. The deal almost died. Now we run our own technical red-team exercises 18 months before any exit process. Never again."*
>
> — CTO, Healthcare AI Portfolio Company

Data gets tested. Systems get pulled apart. But what holds buyers in the process is the story. The AI narrative is what ties the proof to the potential. It's what shows buyers how the system creates sustainable value they can grow. The next step is building a story that holds under diligence, resonates with different buyer types, and drives valuation. This is AI narrative construction.

Chapter 61

A SUCCESSFUL AI EXIT EXECUTION

From Technology Bet to Exit Premium

No one gets a second chance to make a first impression. For PE-backed companies with AI in their story, the stakes are even higher. The last phase means marketing a strong financial profile and proving that the AI capabilities are not only real, but also resilient, transferable, and built to scale.

Buyers are no longer charmed by slides packed with buzzwords. They've seen too many "AI-powered" pitches that crumble under scrutiny. What moves the needle now is preparation, credibility, and a clearly articulated story backed by operational truth.

That's where this framework comes in. It's built to ensure that the AI value created in the growth phase survives the heat of diligence and emerges even stronger post-acquisition. Done right, it leads to a higher multiple, and it positions the company as a platform, not a project.

The Four Dimensions of Exit Success

Valuation Optimization

Understand how different buyers value AI differently. Tailor the story and evidence package to fit what they prize: defensibility, scalability, efficiency, or edge.

Due Diligence Excellence

Sophisticated buyers bring sophisticated questions. Be ready. That means not having clean documentation, and being able to walk through the model governance, data pipelines, AI performance benchmarks, and post-deployment results with fluency and confidence.

Narrative Power

Facts tell. Stories sell. A well-crafted AI narrative connects technical achievements to business outcomes, framed in buyer-relevant language. It doesn't exaggerate; it resonates.

Integration Assurance

The value of AI doesn't stop at close. Buyers want to know if it will hold up, and scale, after Day 1. That means having a roadmap for integration, clear documentation, and offering transitional support or knowledge transfer plans.

Key Success Factors Across All Exit Activities

Preparation Excellence

Begin exit readiness 18–24 months before the target sale. This allows time to strengthen weak spots, clean up technical debt, and build the documentation that will withstand buyer diligence.

Buyer Sophistication

Assume the potential buyers know what they're doing. Most now bring AI experts, either in-house or on retainer, to separate real capability from marketing fluff.

Evidence-Based Positioning

For every claim made, have evidence: dashboards, user metrics, model outputs, customer testimonials, or third-party validation. Confidence without proof won't survive diligence.

Integration Planning

Don't treat integration as a post-close problem. Start mapping potential challenges and dependencies during the exit process. It shows maturity and reduces buyer friction.

The AI Exit Advantage

Companies that execute this phase well win on price, and they win on perception and post-close performance. They walk into the exit process with a story that's not only impressive, but also bulletproof.

In private equity, the only AI that matters is the kind that creates lasting value. Not for one quarter. For the next chapter.

The exit is where your work is tested in public. AI-native systems are harder to fake, but they're also harder to beat. This is where the right build earns its price.

THE JOURNEY BEGINS

Newthistle Consulting LLC

Chapter 62

THE FUTURE WILL NOT WAIT

A Warning to Business Leaders

The idea that you can build a 100-year-old company is gone.

The days of standing still, of cautiously watching from the sidelines, of assuming your market will hold long enough for you to catch up, those days are over.

AI is already reshaping the structure of industries, not just the tools inside them. And it's coming for your business.

Imagine what the future feels like. Imagine being outmaneuvered not by one competitor, but by entire industries that learned to move without waiting for human sign-off. Imagine the frustration of watching your best customers quietly migrate to businesses that can anticipate what they need before they ask. Imagine leadership meetings where you're no longer debating what to do, you're debating whether you can still afford to compete.

Imagine realizing your market has already reorganized around faster, smarter systems, while you were still perfecting last year's playbook.

This isn't a distant future. It's the world your competitors are building right now.

It won't arrive as a single competitor. It will arrive as entire systems that can learn, adapt, and scale faster than you can react. It will arrive as a new generation of businesses that can sense changes in customer behavior before you finish your quarterly review. It will arrive as pricing models, onboarding processes, product features, and supply chains that shift in real time while you are still stuck rerunning last month's reports.

And those businesses will not wait for you to be ready.

In five years, AI will be the infrastructure of competitive businesses. It will no longer be a differentiator. It will simply be the system that keeps you alive. If you haven't built it, you won't be able to buy it fast enough to catch up.

In ten years, the markets will not be split between big and small companies. They will be split between intelligent and static ones. The businesses that succeed will not be people-less, but they will look nothing like the companies we know today. Leadership teams will shrink. Decision cycles will compress into hours, not weeks. Autonomous processes will consume repetitive work that doesn't ask for permission. Sales, support, logistics, and even product innovation will operate inside learning systems that adjust themselves in real time.

People will still matter, but they will matter differently. The winners will be businesses that design their systems to scale intelligence, not just labor. The value of the workforce will come from judgment, creativity, and adaptability, not process execution.

Companies that have built AI as the backbone of their systems will learn faster, move faster, and scale faster than legacy businesses can pivot. They won't just win; they will reframe the game.

And don't assume that long histories guarantee survival. Look at Thomas Cook, a company that pioneered modern travel in the 1840s and survived world wars but collapsed when it failed to modernize its digital booking systems. BlackBerry, once the gold standard in mobile communication was outpaced when the market shifted to touchscreens and app ecosystems. Borders, a leading bookseller missed the e-commerce wave and left the door wide open for Amazon to dominate. These weren't small companies. They weren't short-lived companies. They simply moved too slowly.

Most legacy businesses will not be acquired. They will be ignored.

And the mistake leaders are making right now? They believe they have time. They believe the AI curve will flatten. They believe their customers, their competitors, and their industries will stabilize long enough for them to catch up on their terms. They believe personal relationships with their customers will beat out superior value propositions.

That window has already closed.

The businesses that are building intelligent systems today will compound learning, customer feedback, and operational efficiency over the next five years. The gap will not shrink. It will widen. Waiting is not caution. It's surrender.

AI's impact on the business is already underway. The real question is whether the systems will be built fast enough to make a difference in the next wave of competition.

Leadership teams that delay are making a silent choice: they are betting their competitors will move slowly.

They won't.

The future will not wait.

Final Operator's Log

> *"After three AI-enabled exits over five years, I've learned that the exit phase is where AI either proves its worth or reveals its limitations. The companies that succeed have three things in common: they prove their AI creates measurable business value, they've prepared for sophisticated buyer due diligence, and they've planned for successful post-acquisition integration. The companies that fail have built impressive technology without building the business case, documentation, and transition planning that sophisticated buyers demand. AI exits depend on more than showcasing cool technology. What matters is proving a sustainable competitive advantage that commands premium prices from buyers."*
>
> - Operating Partner, Technology-Focused PE Fund.

In private equity, the exit is the moment everything becomes real. The narrative, the numbers, the diligence prep, the value creation story, it either holds together or it doesn't.

This chapter is a warning. Not a prediction. A reality check.

The businesses that will win the next decade aren't waiting for clarity. They're already building systems that learn, adapt, and operate faster than legacy companies can react. And they're doing it with a level of urgency most leadership teams still underestimate.

But urgency alone isn't a strategy. And panic isn't a plan.

Chapter 63

THE WINDOW IS OPEN

AI Is Here—Now What?

Let's be clear: we are not AI evangelists. We don't believe AI is an instant fix, a cure-all, or the end of human work as we know it.

But we also know it's not a passing trend.

You reaching this point should have made one thing clear: this book wasn't written with rose-tinted glasses. There are no utopian promises, no hype cycles, and no jargon for the sake of sounding smart. Just a clear-eyed view of what it takes to make AI work where it matters most: inside real businesses, under real pressure. No wishful Silicon Valley monologues. We wrote it because AI is real, it's speeding up, and it's already changing how value is captured, protected, and multiplied across the private equity lifecycle.

Yes, there's noise. There's hype. There are many headlines and too few audited results. But walking away from AI because early adopters over-promised, or because a few proof-of-concepts didn't pan out, is like walking away from the internet in 1996 because dial-up was slow.

We've shown throughout this book that AI is not just a tech upgrade. It's a value creation lever. One that, when aligned with strategy and executed with discipline, delivers measurable, tangible, valuation-multiple-impacting outcomes.

Even so, this is difficult work.

Building an AI-native business is hard. It requires coordination across strategy, operations, data, tech, compliance, and culture. It requires cross-functional fluency, uncomfortable decisions, and constant iteration. It's not for tourists or checkbox chasers. It's for leaders.

But that's what makes it an opportunity.

Most companies won't do the work. Some can't. And many will pretend they are while quietly hoping no one asks tough questions. Those who are willing to do the work don't follow the pack; they set the pace. Leadership comes from discipline, not noise.

Yes, AI brings risk. Technical debt if it's deployed without architecture. Execution risk if it's disconnected from the investment thesis. Regulatory exposure if governance is ignored. All real, but manageable. But here's the greater risk: doing nothing.

Waiting for the dust to settle. Hoping the next buyer overlooks the gaps. Assuming competitors will be just as slow to act are not options. In this market, infrastructure compounds. Talent compounds. Execution readiness compounds. AI maturity is the sum of these parts, and without active investment, the gap only grows wider.

Transformation doesn't need to happen overnight. But forward motion does. In the next valuation discussion, the next exit window, the next strategic inflection point, no one will wait for readiness to catch up.

Now is the moment to ask:

- Where does the organization stand in AI understanding, capability, and execution?
- Where can AI create meaningful lift across the portfolio?
- What's required to build institutional fluency before the next decision point arrives?

AI isn't a trend that fades. It's a shift in how value is created, defended, and scaled. The only question is when leadership will stop watching and start acting.

The window is open. Advantage belongs to those who move with focus, not noise. AI is already reshaping the pace of competition, and the organizations that build discipline into their approach will compound those gains over time. Others will hesitate, hoping for clarity that never arrives. By then, the opportunity will belong to someone else. Work starts now.

So what now?

That's where the final chapter begins, not with speculation, but with execution, not with hype, but with hard questions that demand action.

You've seen what AI can do. You've seen what buyers reward. You've seen what happens when companies wait too long.

The future isn't just approaching, it's here. Let's talk about what it takes to move through it with purpose.

Chapter 64

OPERATORS EXECUTIVE SUMMARY

The Playbook in Action

You've read the strategies, seen the pitfalls, and worked through the frameworks. This chapter distills the entire lifecycle into a practical deployment guide you can act on today. Each phase is stripped to its essentials, what to do, when to do it, and how to measure if it's working, with direct links to the companion site tools and playbooks.

This is not a recap of theory. It's the operational spine of The AI Fix for Private Equity, the sequence to follow when the clock is ticking, the board is watching, and the value-creation thesis needs to turn into measurable results. Every phase includes a real-world example from earlier chapters, so you can see how these moves play out in practice. Keep these pages close. They're designed to be the bridge from reading to doing.

Phase 1 – Pre-Deal: Spot the Real AI Advantage

Before the ink is dry, your edge is in what you see that others miss. Use the AI Pre-Deal Intelligence Checklist (www.theaifix.online) to track signals of genuine AI defensibility...

Objective: Identify AI-native value creation before you buy.

Actions:

Use the AI Pre-Deal Intelligence Checklist (Companion Site) to track signals of genuine AI defensibility.

- Validate data ownership and model maturity early, marketing hype can hide fragile AI claims.
- Compare target's AI position against competitors using the Three Applications of AI model (Optimize, Automate, Differentiate).
- Pressure-test leadership team's understanding of AI beyond buzzwords.

- Identify hidden cost levers (COGS, G&A) where AI could materially shift economics post-acquisition.

Example: In one acquisition, "AI-native" claims collapsed under diligence when the target's model turned out to be a public API wrapper, a $200M deal avoided.

Phase 2 – First 100 Days: Build the AI Foundation

Speed is leverage — small wins early earn you the breathing room to make big moves later. Deploy quick-win AI initiatives in high-impact bottlenecks...

Objective: Create early wins and position for scale.

Actions:

- Deploy quick-win AI initiatives in high-impact bottlenecks, revenue cycle time, operational choke points, or defect reduction.
- Establish governance guardrails (Companion Site, AI Governance Framework) to ensure AI is used strategically, not ad hoc.
- Implement dashboards for transparency, enabling both board and management visibility.
- Begin leadership ego assessment using the Ego Mitigation Playbook (Companion Site) to address potential blockers early.
- Map all current processes for AI readiness, flag for automation, optimization, or differentiation potential.

Example: A Fortune 500 retailer used AI-driven demand forecasting in its first 100 days post-acquisition, unlocking $40M in working capital and securing immediate board buy-in.

Phase 3 – Growth Phase: Scale and Differentiate

Efficiency pays the bills; differentiation pays the multiple. Expand automation into multi-step, cross-functional processes...

Objective: Turn AI capability into durable competitive advantage.

Actions:

- Expand automation into multi-step, cross-functional processes, always measure cycle time and margin impact.
- Shift from operational efficiency to customer experience differentiation where AI deepens loyalty and stickiness.
- Integrate AI feedback loops, ensure models improve as data accumulates.
- Track KPIs against your AI Value Compass (Companion Site) to ensure balance across cash, COGS, G&A, and sales levers.
- Keep scanning for horizon threats, AI-native competitors can emerge quickly.

Example: A B2B SaaS portfolio company integrated AI into its onboarding flow, reducing churn by 27% and increasing upsell conversion by 18% within a year.

Phase 4 – Preparing for Exit: Align and Polish

Buyers pay more for a story they can verify.

Audit all AI initiatives, quantify impact, and stage proof points...

Objective: Bake AI defensibility into the equity story.

Actions:

- Audit all AI initiatives — quantify impact on recurring revenue, margins, and market share.
- Stage customer and operational proof points that buyers can verify.
- Remove "single point of failure" risks in AI delivery or governance.
- Link prestige and recognition to AI milestones to ensure leadership is motivated through the sale process.
- Use the Exit Premium Playbook (Companion Site) to benchmark against premium vs discounted exit outcomes.

Example: A tech services portfolio company reframed its AI-powered logistics engine as defensible IP, which added 1.5x to its revenue multiple during sale negotiations.

Phase 5 – Exit Premium Playbook: Maximize Valuation

Premium exits are built, not wished for.

Present AI as a growth engine with defensible IP and data, not just as a cost-saving tool...

Objective: Turn AI capability into a valuation multiplier.

Actions:

- Present AI not as a cost-saving tool but as a growth engine with defensible IP, data, and customer lock-in.
- Showcase examples where AI created competitive advantage that would be hard to replicate post-acquisition.
- Structure the management presentation to lead with strategic outcomes, not technical detail.
- Anticipate buyer due diligence questions on AI, have governance, ethics, and compliance answers ready.
- Use Premium vs Discounted Outcomes Matrix (Companion Site) to identify where to strengthen before buyer scrutiny.

Example: A $500M enterprise software company's sale was discounted by 20% after buyers discovered its AI engine relied on unlicensed datasets, a preventable loss.

Key Reminders

- Use the Tools – Every phase has a checklist or playbook linked on the companion site.
- Sequence Matters – Skipping early diligence steps undermines later exit positioning.
- Egos Can Break This – If leadership resists AI integration, address it before it costs you valuation.

Final Approach: From Plan to Proof

You have the chart, the checklists, and a flight plan from pre-deal to exit. The playbooks are simple enough to use under pressure, rigorous enough to stand up in diligence. You are not guessing, you are executing.

Momentum starts small, then compounds. Pick the next constraint, apply the right tool, measure what moves, keep what works, retire what doesn't. Good governance keeps you out of the headlines, clear dashboards keep you out of the dark, steady cadence keeps you out of trouble.

Build capability while you build results. Pair experienced operators with AI support, give less experienced people real reps with safety rails, capture the judgment behind every decision. When people move on, the system keeps flying.

Buyers pay for proof, not promises. Keep your trail of evidence current, revenue lift, margin expansion, faster cycle times, lower risk. Package it so a skeptical buyer can verify it in an afternoon.

Close this book, open the playbooks, and get to work. You have everything you need to turn this thesis into outcomes, and to earn the premium that follows.

www.ingramcontent.com/pod-product-compliance
Lightning Source LLC
LaVergne TN
LVHW050929210926
848482LV00013B/585